George Meredith

Twayne's English Authors Series

Herbert Sussman, Editor

Northeastern University

TEAS 434

GEORGE MEREDITH
(1828–1909)
Photograph by Harold Roller, 1888
Reproduced courtesy of Morris Library,
University of Delaware

George Meredith

By Renate Muendel

West Chester University

Twayne Publishers
A Division of G.K. Hall & Co. • *Boston*

For Jan,
friend and ally
of the Comic Spirit

George Meredith

Renate Muendel

Copyright © 1986 by G.K. Hall & Co.
All Rights Reserved
Published by Twayne Publishers
A Division of G.K. Hall & Co.
70 Lincoln Street
Boston, Massachusetts 02111

Copyediting supervised by Lewis DeSimone
Book production by Elizabeth Todesco
Book design by Barbara Anderson

Typeset in 11 pt. Garamond
by P&M Typesetting, Inc., Waterbury, Connecticut

Printed on permanent/durable acid-free paper
and bound in the United States of America

Library of Congress Cataloging in Publication Data

Muendel, Renate.
  George Meredith.

  (Twayne's English authors series; TEAS 434)
  Bibliography: p. 140
  Includes index.
  1. Meredith, George, 1828–1909—Criticism and
interpretation.   I. Title.   II. Series.
PR5014.M84   1986   823'.8   86-12110
ISBN 0-8057-6932-3

Contents

About the Author

Renate Muendel received her undergraduate education at the Universities of Goettingen and Tuebingen, West Germany. She has an M.A. in German from Columbia University and an M.A. and Ph.D. in English from the University of Delaware. She teaches at West Chester University and is presently working on a study of Mrs. Humphry Ward.

Preface

George Meredith's poems and fiction still lack a firm place in the history of English literature. Never a commercial success, he was in his own time rejected by mainstream critics but extravagantly praised by a number of young intellectuals and fellow writers. To his admirers the adjective *Meredithian* denoted a lively and challenging creativity, and some of them went so far as to compare him to Shakespeare. At his death in 1909 he had come to be considered, by the intellectual elite, the epitome of the Victorian man of letters. The high claims of his coterie were bound to evoke a negative reaction, which came with the end of World War I. By the 1920s *Meredithian* signified pretentiousness of style and intellectual humbug, a judgment that led to a general neglect of his work over the next fifty years. Even today Meredith is known to academics and readers of Victorian fiction for only two of his thirteen novels, *The Egoist* and *The Ordeal of Richard Feverel*.

In a perceptive essay at Meredith's centenary in 1928, Virginia Woolf asserted that his novels "must inevitably rise from time to time into view; his work must inevitably be disputed and discussed."[1] Such a revival of critical interest in Meredith has occurred in the last twenty years. It is now generally acknowledged that he contributed significantly to the development of the English novel, combining in his work a self-conscious adaptation of earlier conventions and an exploration of narrative methods pointing toward twentieth-century fiction. Along with Henry James he established the novel's claim to high art, enriching the genre with an extraordinary flexibility of language and pre-Freudian awareness of subconscious states of mind.

At the center of Meredith's work is a radically new concept of realism—a rejection of the linear and consistent in favor of the complex, shifting, and paradoxical. This concept, suggested even in his first prose work, *The Shaving of Shagpat* (1855), but explicitly set forth in *Diana of the Crossways* (1885), informs his plots and characterizations, although neither consistently nor always successfully. It is also reflected in his self-conscious attitude toward the novel as a genre. Meredith looked at his material, his audience, and his authorship with a peculiar mixture of ironic detachment and vigorous personal commitment. He underscored this stance by use of an extravagant rhetoric composed of witty epigrams, proliferating metaphors, a skillful imitation of upper-class speech, and a syntax often strikingly un-English.

This study sees Meredith working with recalcitrant material—exhausted literary traditions, the shallowness of contemporary reading taste, the inertia and spiritual vacuity of English society, and his own ambivalent feelings about class and sexual divisions. In the three chapters on his fiction, I have focused on the experimental nature of his work, his aggressive attempts to combine contradictory elements, and his pleas for self-knowledge and charity in communal life. I have included discussion of minor as well as major novels in order to show how they successively reexamine both novelistic conventions and his central social and philosophical concerns through changes in emphasis and focus. A chapter on Meredith's poetry, preceding analysis of the novels, demonstrates how his astonishing creative energy worked in an affirmation of a post-Darwinian worldview that allows full play to dialectics and ambiguities but assumes the possibility of a correct "Reading of Life."

Over the last twenty years, excellent editions of Meredith's verse and letters as well as several fine studies of the poet and storyteller have argued persuasively for a new look at this sophisticated artist. I am indebted to them all in more ways than the footnotes can acknowledge. To friends and teachers, particularly Jerry Beasley and Barbara Gates, I am grateful for incisive and stimulating conversations on Meredith and the Victorian novel in general. Herbert Sussman, my editor, helped me clarify my points and keep my reader in mind. My family was unvaryingly patient and encouraging. My deepest gratitude goes to my mentor and dear friend Anna Janney De Armond, for her unfailing kindness, thoroughness, and intellectual acuity in her service as sounding board and critical reader.

Renate Muendel

West Chester University

Chronology

Chapter One

Life

In 1901, when George Meredith had long been a respected writer and famous personality, his friend Edward Clodd assisted him in filling out a national census sheet. Asked about his place of birth, Meredith tried to hedge the answer: "Well, put Hampshire." When his friend objected, he suggested, "Near Petersfield." He was equally evasive about his occupation; instead of "author" he inserted "has private means."[1]

A student of Meredith's life sees more than a crotchety old man's reticence in this episode. Throughout his life Meredith was extremely chary with information about his past; it was impossible for him to acknowledge his background as a tailor's son, and he anxiously concealed any details about his first marriage. Even his status as an author did not meet his unqualified approval, as the episode shows—although he felt honored to be called a poet. Poets, after all, could be found among undisputed gentlemen, whereas authors made their living by writing, worried about the financial results of a negative review, and were devastated if Mudie's lending library for whatever petty reason rejected their novels. For Meredith, poetry and prose were the means of expressing ideas he considered vitally important; that they also provided his livelihood—were, in fact, the only major means of providing it, since he had no independent fortune—was an unwelcome and unstressed fact of his life.

Like Dickens, Meredith tried valiantly to keep the dark aspects of his past from intruding into the bright picture of the present; but like Dickens's experience of the blacking factory, they appear in various disguises throughout his fiction. Of all major Victorian writers, Meredith is, next to Dickens, the most autobiographical. Thinly veiled, the stigma of his lower-middle-class background, the failure of his father to provide adequately for a promising son, and the shattered dream of his first marriage furnish plot elements for his novels and images for his ideas. His fiction is the record of his struggle to free himself from the personal pain of his past by objectifying it, transforming his personal perplexities into universal paradoxes. The intellectual combativeness characterizing his writings is directed not only against his complacent British readers but also against his own tendency toward pettiness and snobbery as well as his intermittent failure to see beyond his personal tragedy.

For many reasons Meredith saw himself as an outsider entitled to hold up the mirror to his contemporaries. He was partly justified in this role; but it was just that—a role by which he could impose a healing order on the tumult of his own lacerated feelings as well as preach reason to his fellowmen. In fact, the very stance of the alienated writer and isolated sage was one that Meredith shared with many other Victorian authors. Admittedly, he had a larger range of vision and a more strident tone than most. Except for George Eliot, none was as cosmopolitan and as intellectually energetic as he, and his rhetorical combativeness surpasses that of all others except Carlyle. Yet both in his concerns and in his strategies Meredith was a representative figure of his culture; and his life and works, blending into each other at times poignantly, at times irritatingly, afford us a vivid insight into the situation of a Victorian "man of ideas."

Early Years

George Meredith was born on 12 February 1828, the only child of Augustus Urmston Meredith and his wife, Jane, née Macnamara. Augustus was a naval outfitter and tailor at Portsmouth, but only by economic necessity. His own father, George's grandfather, who was to appear, thinly disguised, as the protagonist's flamboyant father in Meredith's early novel *Evan Harrington,* had been a highly respected tradesman. He had developed his tailoring shop into an important establishment in town, and because of his handsome appearance and social acumen, he had not only been among the leading citizens of Portsmouth but had also held his own among the county squires. But Melchizedek Meredith had not passed on either his geniality or his common sense to his son, Augustus, who grew up with unrealistic social ambitions heightened by the fact that his four sisters had all made advantageous matches. When the "Great Mel" died and his business needed a shrewd, down-to-earth manager, Augustus, with his pretensions to gentility, his extravagant tastes, and his dislike of the tailor's craft, was clearly not the right man.[2] Under his reluctant management, the Meredith establishment gradually declined in fi-

nancial solidity. Even Augustus's marriage in 1823 to Jane Macnamara, an apparently sensible young woman of respectable middle-class
background, could only slow down the process, and Jane died ten
years later.

George Meredith was five years old at the time of his mother's
death. To judge from accounts of relatives and his own reminiscences,
he was not much affected by it, although the fact that he was a very
fearful child and could not bear to be left alone suggests a sense of
loss. It is striking, however, that in his novels the mother-child relationship appears only in the most tenuous, abstract form; whereas
father-son and father-daughter relationships are crucial to many of his
plots, mothers are usually either dead (and unmissed) or shadowy
figures in the background. Meredith's sensitivity to female psychology clearly does not derive from the un-self-conscious intimate knowledge a child absorbs from a long unbroken life with his mother. But
when questioned on this point by Alice Brandreth, who wrote her
Memories of George Meredith later as Lady Butcher, he replied, "It is
my mother that is in me."[3]

In spite of the economic decline of the family business, George
grew up with the same idea of social superiority his father had nour-
ished. He was rather isolated from playmates; the children of the
tradespeople in his neighborhood called him "Gentleman George" because of his prettiness, his aloofness, and his lack of interest in their
games.[4] In his mind he held the dream of a glorious royal Celtic ancestry—a myth that had originated with the "Great Mel" and was
passed on to him through his father. It is true that Meredith's background was partly Welsh and partly Irish, but there is no evidence
whatever of any royal ancestry in his family.[5] While Augustus may
have held on to this myth in order to compensate psychologically for
the actual bleakness of his circumstances, it played a more productive
role in the formation of George's mind: along with nostalgia and hau-
teur it fostered a sense of displacement he was later able to turn into
irony against his own social pretensions. Meredith was always to remain partial to the Welsh and the Irish, ascribing to them—in typical nineteenth-century ethnological fashion—the "Celtic" virtues of
rhetorical vivacity, affinity with nature, and sympathy with women.
But the illusion of a royal ancestry he exorcised with superb imaginative wit in his novel *Harry Richmond*.

At the age of eleven Meredith lost the companionship of his im-
provident father, who had to declare bankruptcy and live thereafter as

a modest tailor first in London and later in Capetown, South Africa. For a while George stayed in Portsmouth, possibly with some more prosperous relatives, and then was sent to a boarding school. Details about this part of his life are so few that we do not even know the locality of the school except that it was at the seashore.[6] Apparently its academic program made little impression on the boy; one of his most vivid recollections in later years was becoming acquainted with the *Arabian Nights,* a book that was to play a major role in the growth of his imagination, as his own first prose writing testifies, but that certainly had no place in the curriculum of this narrowly traditional school.

In 1842 Meredith left England for Germany, where for two years he attended the Moravian school at Neuwied on the Rhine. The daily contact with the gentle, educationally enlightened Brethren helped him overcome a typical British parochialism. It converted his snobbism into a more detached and critical interest in the social system, awakened a romantic love of nature, and fostered a sense of chivalry and fair play. Neuwied saved him from becoming an insufferable prig or a merely fashionable author. It taught him a healthy respect for the physical realities of human and natural life—the students were encouraged to take long hikes and to associate with the townspeople. For the rest of his life Meredith would insist that a truly admirable character not only thinks and acts nobly but also enjoys physical vigor, understands the processes of nature, and is on easy terms with his fellowmen of all classes. Above all, Neuwied laid the groundwork for his detestation of pretentiousness, and it provided him with ideals that would prevent him from adopting the stance of the worldly-wise cynic, however bitterly he often felt about his circumstances.

First Marriage and Early Literary Career

In 1846, eighteen months after he had returned from Neuwied,[7] Meredith was articled to Richard Stephen Charnock, a young London solicitor, for training in the legal profession. Since Charnock was a sociable, easygoing man with an interesting circle of friends, the following years helped the tailor's son shed any remaining social awkwardness and acquainted him with the scientific, literary, and philosophical topics under discussion among educated men. Charnock became his mentor—not in the study of law, the pursuit of which was soon abandoned, but in social and intellectual sophistication.

In this circle Meredith met Mary Ellen Nicolls, a widow seven years older than he and the mother of a five-year-old girl.[8] Mary Nicolls was a brilliantly witty and spirited woman, who enlivened the Charnock circle with sharp satire and passionate emotional outbursts. Meredith fell thoroughly in love with her. At the age of twenty-one, without training in any profession, without a social position, and with only a very small estate by maternal inheritance, he proposed to her with a persistence she could not withstand. They were married in August 1849, and after a honeymoon along the Rhine, they moved to Weybridge, Surrey, where they lived close to Mary's father, the writer Thomas Love Peacock.[9]

The young couple planned to support themselves by writing. Meredith had already contributed poems, articles, and translations to a manuscript magazine circulating in the Charnock group, and *Chambers's Edinburgh Journal* published his poem "Chillianwallah," inspired by a battle in the Second Sikh War. Poems by Meredith appeared in Dickens's *Household Words;* he contributed to other periodicals as well. His first volume of poetry, entitled *Poems,* came out in 1851. It was an important venture for Meredith, since here he presented himself to an audience accustomed to Tennyson and Browning as well as a host of minor postromantics aptly termed "Spasmodics." Meredith had tried to find his own voice: his delight in nature and joyful confidence in the rightness of natural processes were often expressed in unusual techniques of rhyme and meter. Although the volume gained him exposure and some laudatory reviews, especially from fellow poets such as Tennyson, it did not sell, and since Meredith had paid the publication costs of sixty pounds himself, his financial situation deteriorated badly.

Over the next few years life became increasingly difficult for the couple. They moved several times, finally settling with her father, who found it vexing to live with his mercurial son-in-law. Meredith contributed mediocre poems to *Household Words* and other magazines; Mary, plagued with almost continuous miscarriages, made more money by writing an article on gourmet cooking to which Meredith and her father, who was much interested in good food and classical recipes, contributed. In 1853 she gave birth to a healthy son, but the strained circumstances of the Peacock-Meredith household allowed little joy.

Finally, Meredith resigned himself to writing prose as more remunerative than composing poetry. But his first venture in fiction, an allegorical fantasy reminiscent of the *Arabian Nights* and called *The Shaving of Shagpat: An Arabian Entertainment,* which Chapman and Hall published in 1855, was met with puzzlement by most critics and widespread indifference by the reading public.[10] Since Meredith had worked long over this story, the public's lack of understanding discouraged him. Another narrative, this time a romantic legend set in Cologne and entitled *Farina,* was published by Smith, Elder in 1857; again it met with little financial success, though some respected critics gave it qualified praise. Among them was George Eliot, who at this time still wrote reviews for the *Westminster Review* and the *Leader* under her real name, Marian Evans.

Meanwhile, Meredith's marriage was coming to an end. Frustrated by the poverty of their lives and impatient with her husband's impractical aspirations, Mary eloped with a young Pre-Raphaelite painter, Henry Wallis, and in 1859 gave birth to his child. When she accompanied her lover to Italy, Meredith took charge of his little son, Arthur, then five years old, and refused to see his wife again, even though she returned to England alone, unhappy, and apparently hoping for a reconciliation. He had been bitterly humiliated, but we can guess his feelings only from the poetry and fiction he wrote in the following years; neither in letters nor in conversation did he give vent to his emotions. It is easy for us today to recognize the flaws that doomed the marriage from the start: two brilliantly gifted people, witty, temperamental, ambitious, were worn down by dire external circumstances and the pressure of their competing natures. But for Meredith, this failure temporarily shook the foundations of his trust in nature. Taking care of his young son and probing his tragedy in prose and verse helped him overcome the crisis; for a while, however, he played the misogynist, employing only manservants to look after Arthur and writing to a friend, Bonaparte Wyse:

Women, my dear fellow, can occasionally be fine creatures, if they fall into good hands. Physically they neighbor the vegetable, and morally the animal creation; and they are, therefore, chemically good for men, and to be away from them is bad for that strange being who, because they serve his uses, calls them angels.[11]

In 1859 Chapman and Hall published Meredith's first novel, *The Ordeal of Richard Feverel,* which had grown very obviously out of his personal tragedy and contains a number of autobiographical elements, such as his concern about the upbringing of his boy.[12] Apart from this aspect, Meredith was keenly interested in making the genre of the novel do what he thought was the chief function of respectable writing: promote self-knowledge, "close knowledge of our fellows," and "discernment of the laws of existence" (*Letters*, 2:876). With such lofty aspirations, he was chagrined to find that his first full-fledged novel elicited little critical praise (although both the *Times* and the *Spectator* published favorable reviews). Yet more damaging than critical neglect, Mudie's lending library banned it from its purchasing list because of a seduction scene considered too risqué.

Fortunately, Meredith had an understanding and steadfast supporter in his publisher, and although *Richard Feverel* did nothing to enhance his financial state, other work with Chapman and Hall began to give him a small but regular income. He wrote poems for a new weekly periodical, *Once a Week*, and read manuscripts submitted to the publishing house. In this latter capacity, which he kept up for most of his life, he made a number of important discoveries and decisions for Chapman and Hall. He was the anonymous reader and adviser for both Thomas Hardy and George Gissing. In 1869, after Hardy had submitted his first novel, *The Poor Man and the Lady*, Meredith turned it down. He counseled Hardy to concentrate on plot rather than social criticism, a suggestion Hardy interpreted as "more sensationalism" and followed up with *Desperate Remedies*, a highly improbable tale of mystery and murder. Meredith accepted Gissing's second novel, *The Unclassed*, for publication in 1883, afterward advising Gissing to stay with lower-class protagonists. He rejected Samuel Butler's *Erewhon* as too philosophical for a general audience. He also declined Mrs. Henry Wood's *East Lynne*, which later became tremendously popular; in this case, as in several others, his high standards of workmanship and intellectual demands of fiction caused a loss of profit for his company. But throughout their association, Chapman and Hall respected his judgment, and several writers—Hardy and Gissing among them—left testimonies to his kindness and helpfulness in their early careers.

While he was writing his second novel, *Evan Harrington* (1860), Meredith was in love with the teenage daughter of aristocratic neighbors, the Duff Gordons. He had known Janet Duff Gordon when she was a little girl who called him "my poet" and had met her again after the breakdown of his marriage. His precarious financial situation and the fact that his wife was still alive in 1860 prevented Meredith from entertaining any serious hopes about winning Janet; instead, she became the frank, spunky, and independent-minded heroine of *Evan Harrington,* Rose Jocelyn—a transformation Janet proudly acknowledged.

Although *Evan Harrington* was a much more conventional and immaculately proper book, it received less attention than *Richard Feverel* had. But Meredith was branching out into other literary occupations, and financially at least he was not hurt by the public's indifference. He became an editorial writer for the *Ipswich Journal,* a strictly Tory paper owned by one of his friends, and a "gentleman reader" to a wealthy old lady who liked to discuss literature with him. Although he had to go up to London regularly, he found great pleasure in his little house in Surrey (Copsham Cottage, near Esher) and a constant source of refreshment in the surrounding countryside. He made new friends, whom he invited to his home and enticed to strenuous, invigorating rambles. Among his acquaintances was Francis Burnand, who gives us a lively description of the writer at this period:

George Meredith never merely walked, never lounged; he strode, he took giant strides. He had on a soft, shapeless wide-awake, a sad-coloured flannel shirt, with low open collar turned over a brilliant scarlet neckerchief tied in loose sailor's knot; no waistcoat; knickerbockers, grey stockings, and the most serviceable laced boots, which evidently meant business in pedestrianism; crisp, curly, brownish hair, ignorant of parting; a fine brow, quick observant eyes, greyish—if I remember rightly;—beard and moustache, a trifle lighter than the hair. A splendid head; a memorable personality. Then his sense of humor, his cynicism, and his absolutely boyish enjoyment of mere fun, of any pure and simple absurdity. His laugh was something to hear; it was of short duration, but it was a roar; it set you off—nay, he himself, when much tickled, would laugh till he cried (it didn't take long to get to the crying), and then he would struggle with himself, hand to open mouth, to prevent another outburst. [13]

In 1861, on his return from a vacation with his son in Switzerland and Italy, Meredith found that his wife had come back to England, where she died in October. Her death caused him to reexamine the stormy course of their marriage and to cast his thoughts into a sequence of sonnetlike stanzas. The result is "Modern Love," next to *The Egoist* the best known and today most admired of Meredith's works. Since its main topic is conjugal infidelity, it was not well received by the public, but Meredith gained a valuable new friend in

Algernon Swinburne, who wrote a letter to the *Spectator* in defense of the poem. For a while Meredith associated frequently with him and with the Pre-Raphaelites, but it was not a very steady friendship: Meredith himself was very touchy, but at the same time liked to needle his companions mercilessly. In addition, he was unusually fastidious. An attempt at a communal menage with Swinburne and the Rossetti brothers, Dante Gabriel and William Michael, lasted only a few months and was marked by frequent quarrels among these temperamentally incompatible spirits.

Second Marriage and Middle Years

In 1864, at the age of thirty-six, Meredith found new happiness in marriage with Marie Vulliamy, a pleasant, gentle woman of twenty-four who had no literary ambitions of her own and devoted herself entirely to her husband's interests. She was of French background, a fine piano player, and pretty in an unassuming way. She also had an excellent sense of humor and an apparently vast reservoir of patience and tact, which enabled her to deal diplomatically with both her husband and those he annoyed by his sarcasm. Meredith's marriage was undeniably happy, and his family life consoled him when his professional success was disturbingly slow to materialize.

The couple set up house in Flint Cottage, near Box Hill, Surrey, which he loved intensely for its beautiful country. Lady Butcher presents an amusing picture of the "madman" of Box Hill in her *Memories of George Meredith:* when she and her cousin—both still children— roused the poet to watch the sun rise, "in a miraculously short time Mr. M. joined us, slightly clad, his nightshirt thrust into brown trousers, and his bare feet into leather slippers, no hat on his head, twisting his stick, and summoning his brown retriever dog. He started to walk very fast up the steep grass incline of Box Hill, very easy for him to climb in those vigorous days."[14] Her main impression of the morning jaunt, however, was not Meredith's physical energy but his intellectual liveliness. That this liveliness often took the form of merciless teasing is shown in another of her observations:

Meredith used to think out problems while he talked to his wife and sons, and sometimes, without enough consideration, would let the lightning of his wit play about their heads. He did the same to all of us, but we only experienced it occasionally, it merely amused and interested us; but I often admired the wise if somewhat pained silence with which Mrs. Meredith followed her wayward husband's varying moods, as she listened to his experiments in sarcasm.[15]

Family obligations made it necessary for Meredith to write novels at briefer intervals. *Emilia in England* (later called *Sandra Belloni*) appeared in 1864, *Rhoda Fleming* in 1865, and *Vittoria* in 1867. During the Italian War in 1866 Meredith was sent to the northern Italian front as a special correspondent for the *Morning Post*. Although the war was over in a few weeks and he never really got to the front lines during an ongoing battle, he made use of the opportunity to acquaint himself with the countryside; *Vittoria,* which is set in Lombardy and the Piedmont, testifies rather oppressively to his thoroughness in his explorations of locale and customs. Reluctant to return to England after his short Continental stay, Meredith spent a few days in Vienna, and here he met Leslie Stephen, with whom he would remain friends throughout his life.

Stephen, the editor of the *Cornhill Magazine* in which Meredith's next novel, *The Adventures of Harry Richmond,* appeared in 1871, shared Meredith's interests in progressive and positivist ideas. Like the writer, he was also an enthusiastic hiker and climber (Vernon Whitford of *The Egoist* is modeled after him) and spent many days tramping around the Surrey countryside in Meredith's company. Other important acquaintances and friends Meredith had made included a young man of aristocratic background and a highly idealistic nature, Capt. Frederick Maxse, who had won acclaim as a very young naval commander in the Crimean War and thereafter had involved himself in politics. Maxse, a Radical despite his privileged birth, had stood for a parliamentary election in 1868 and enlisted Meredith's help in the campaign. While Meredith sympathized with his views, he had little taste for actual political life; moreover, he saw the excesses of political fervor in both the Radical and the Conservative parties, and particularly the excesses of an idealistic temperament in his friend. Maxse became the model of the protagonist in *Beauchamp's Career,* published in 1875.

In 1877 Meredith made use of a different opportunity to speak to his public: he delivered a lecture at the London Institute with the title "The Idea of Comedy and the Uses of the Comic Spirit." The lecture set forth his conceptions of comedy, human progress, and the equality of the sexes, all of which play central roles in his work. The same ideas appear—very explicitly—in *The Egoist,* published in 1879, twenty years after *Richard Feverel.* This novel, Meredith's most skillful and witty celebration of the power of comedy, has done more than any other to familiarize his name to a later generation of readers.

The Egoist was published by Kegan Paul and ushered in a period of unmistakable, though limited, popular success for the author. But his own worldview was darkening. In 1881 he suffered the first symptoms of a debilitating neurological disorder—locomotor ataxia— which eventually forced him to give up his beloved long rambles through the Surrey countryside. Shortly afterward, his hearing deteriorated. His lively and frequently acerbic temperament was not given to patient suffering, in spite of an often professed "joyful resignation" to nature's course. Visitors to Flint Cottage—and there were now more and more, from both England and the Continent, who came to pay their respects to the admired author—found him to be irritable and impatient, opinionated, forever fixed on new theories concerning his diet and medical treatment, and an amazingly patriarchal family man. His wife had borne him two children, whom he brought up along traditional lines; Arthur, his son by Mary Nicolls, lived mostly on the Continent, disappointing his father because he was neither intellectual nor very practical, and destined to die young from tuberculosis.

Meredith published another volume of poetry in 1883. Called *Poems and Lyrics of the Joy of Earth,* it collected various poems from earlier appearances in magazines, but many significant pieces were new, among them a number of fine sonnets and long philosophical poems. With this volume, Meredith made a name for himself as a poet. But as had happened so often, critical attention, though strong, was marked by lack of understanding and complaints about the obscurity of his language. It convinced him more than ever of the British public's stupidity; indeed, an admirer wanting to secure his goodwill could do no better than to declare his poems better than his prose. His high opinion of poetry in general—not just his own— found expression in his novel of 1885, *Diana of the Crossways.*

Here, as in his preceding novel, *The Tragic Comedians,* an actual incident provided the kernel of his plot. Meredith modeled Diana Warwick's troubled history after that of Caroline Norton, who in the 1830s and 1840s had been associated with political leaders, involved in a lawsuit brought against Prime Minister Melbourne by her husband, and implicated in the premature revelation of the Corn Laws repeal by the press. Mrs. Norton, whom Meredith had occasionally met at the Duff Gordons', where she was a favorite friend of the family, was famous for her beauty and wit and had published a number of poems and novels. Diana resembles her in these features and also in her Irish ancestry. It is not astonishing that the novel met with widespread public interest and proved a thorough financial success for its author and its publisher. It went quickly through several editions, but after a relative of Mrs. Norton protested against its hints of scandal, Meredith made sure to spell out explicitly that it was to be taken purely as fiction. Public interest was not reduced by this disclaimer.

Later Years: The Sage of Box Hill

The commercial success of *Diana* induced Chapman and Hall to bring out a uniform edition of Meredith's works, an undertaking that required some revising, shortening, and renaming. But Meredith, although gratified by the critical attention this edition finally bestowed on him, was undergoing a difficult ordeal that put to the test all his proclaimed joyful acceptance of natural processes. In 1885 his wife died of cancer after a long and painful struggle. A number of poems coming out of this experience and collected in *A Reading of Earth* bear witness to his suffering and fortitude. His own health also steadily declined; deafness and his inability to take walks particularly troubled him. But there were compensations: more and more visitors, among them Robert Louis Stevenson, Hardy, and Gissing, flocked to Box Hill to hear the now famous author talk.

Ballads and Poems of Tragic Life, a new collection of poems, was published by Macmillan in 1887. Again the reviews were mixed, with the usual strictures on his difficult style. Meredith liked to turn away from such unpleasant reactions to the interest and frequent admiration his work elicited in America. Faced with what he considered the moral bankruptcy and mental decline of his compatriots, he found in Americans his hope for the future. The Germans also impressed him, since he admired their energy, intellectual vigor, and realistic approach to political questions. He dearly loved the French—among his fictional characters he was most fond of Renée de Croisnel in *Beauchamp's Career*—but in the Franco-Prussian War he grudgingly admitted that the French defeat was deserved; indeed, he hoped, as he stated in "France: December 1870," that this defeat would lead to a moral renewal of France. For his own country he had little hope. In the Boer War he was disgusted with the English and often expressed his admiration for the Boers. He felt strongly about the need for Irish Home Rule. Politically, he was a Liberal, with radical leanings, and in later years, when he sometimes consented to give newspaper interviews, he vigorously voiced his distaste for the indolence and shoddiness that he felt pervaded Conservative British politics.

The book most vividly displaying Meredith's concern with the complacent and mercenary spirit of British social life is *One of Our Conquerors,* which Meredith first published serially in the *Fortnightly,* a radical review under his friend John Morley, in 1890–91. Since its protagonist, an immensely successful but deluded businessman, is benevolent and likable, Meredith had hoped that his downfall would be troubling to the reader. But like most of Meredith's novels, this one did not find many readers to touch or trouble. In execution, particularly in its tendency to digress and its frantic whirls of allusions and images, it set a new record of alienation between the author and the reading public. As the *Daily Chronicle* saw it, "Mr. Meredith grows more and more trying. He seems to take a Satanic delight in wrapping simplicity in as many fantastic coverings as he can devise."[16] But in 1908 a French admirer of Meredith, who visited the sage at Box Hill, was perplexed to hear him assert that *One of Our Conquerors* had been meant to vex the critics, that it was difficult and obscure precisely to confound the reviewers, whom Meredith could not forgive their earlier indifference.[17]

Two other novels, the last Meredith completed, avoided his extreme pessimism and the stylistic difficulties of *One of Our Conquerors. Lord Ormond and His Aminta* came out in 1894, followed by *The Amazing Marriage* in 1895. Both novels were greeted with general relief and praise, although the fairy-tale elements and improbabilities of *The Amazing Marriage* led one critic to call it "The Amazing Baby."[18] In this novel, Meredith particularly indulged in his love for the Welsh character, and it is significant that the one unfinished work that was found among his papers after his death, and on which he had been intermittently at work from *Harry Richmond* on, is entitled *Celt and Saxon,* proof that his interest in the racial qualities of English characters was strong throughout his career.

Despite his preoccupation with novel writing, complicated by the fact that he switched publishers late in life (from Chapman and Hall to Constable in 1895) and that a collected edition of his books came out also in the United States,[19] Meredith's enduring passion was his poetry. He continued writing and publishing volumes of verse throughout his later years: *A Reading of Earth* (1888), *The Empty Purse* (1892), *Odes in Contribution to the Song of French History* (1898), and *A Reading of Life* (1901). In poetry and fiction as well as in his daily life he cultivated the role of the sage. Like the old Goethe, whom he revered, he was enchanted with a number of young female admirers and vacillated between posing as their kindly adviser and intimating a somewhat less avuncular feeling toward them. With his male visitors he strove to uphold an appearance of vitality, energy, and intellectual keenness. His tendency to monopolize the conversation, noticeable throughout his life, was naturally reinforced by his deafness; most of his guests sat through his monologues with a mixture of timidity— for he could still be cutting when he failed to perceive respect or alertness in his listeners—and admiration of his verbal fireworks.

Some of his visitors detected artificiality in his display of brilliance. Henry James called him "a charming, a quite splendid and rather strange, Exhibition, so content itself to *be* one."[20] Desmond MacCarthy visited him in 1901 and described his talk as "full of flourishes and his enunciation grandiose, as though he loved the sound of his own words. . . . He talked with a kind of swagger."[21] But none went away without feeling moved by the old man's courageous effort to minimize the impression of his illness, and he spoke honestly when he asserted that he took "as keen an interest in the movement of life as ever."[22] To G. K. Chesterton and H. G. Wells he even outlined the idea of a highly farcical story, hoping that one of them would follow it up. To the very end he was opinionated about politics and excited about any possible sign of human progress, whether in law, morals, or technology.

Despite his misgivings about the British reading public, the old Meredith had become a "grand old man of letters." Not only did he receive the Order of Merit; he was also honored extensively on his eightieth birthday on 12 February 1908. Both King Edward and President Theodore Roosevelt sent messages, and 250 prominent men from both sides of the Atlantic signed a testimonial document. Of his earliest friends, only Swinburne was still alive, but a new generation of writers and thinkers, among them Clement Shorter, W. D. Howells, Henry Adams, George Trevelyan, W. E. Henley, and Alice Meynell, saw in him the nineteenth century at its most venerable.

Meredith died on 18 May 1909, in his home on Box Hill after a short illness, very much as his great model Goethe had died; he caught a cold on a raw day in spring, the season to which both he and Goethe looked for renewal of body and soul. Meredith accepted serenely the inevitable outcome. Because he had always mocked the custom of the British to bury even their agnostic writers in the Poets' Corner, and because he was really too much of a freethinker even for the most liberal clergy, only a memorial service was held at Westminster Abbey. He was buried in the Dorking cemetery next to his wife, under a simple tombstone inscribed with words from one of his poems:

> Our life is but a little holding, lent
> To do a mighty labour. We are one
> With heaven and the stars when it is spent
> To serve God's aim. Else die we with the Sun.

Chapter Two
Meredith's Poetry

To the general reader, Meredith is known as a novelist, not as a poet. Only a few of his poems are accessible in modern anthologies, and only "Modern Love" appears occasionally in critical discussions of Victorian verse. Meredith would not have been surprised by this neglect of his poetry because he found the audience of his own time imperceptive and indifferent to his poetic achievement, but he would have been distressed since he always hoped for a more understanding future generation. He considered his poetry superior to his prose fiction. He had an exalted concept of poetry in general; in a letter of 1887 he wrote:

The treasure of verse is where thought embraces feeling, as the man the woman. Then you have joined the highest in mind with the deepest in nature. That is why Poetry is above philosophy: it is the voice of essential man before the Gods. (*Letters,* 2:862)

That he considered poetry the choicest flowering of the human spirit is reflected in his lifelong commitment to the writing of verse as well as in the fact that the high purpose of poetry forms a prominent theme in many of his own poems.

Meredith wrote poetry for more than seventy years. His first published poem, "Chillianwallah," commemorating a battle of the Second Sikh War in 1849, appeared in *Chambers's Edinburgh Journal* when he was barely twenty-one; even earlier unpublished verses have been preserved in manuscript. His last published poem was again commemorative: an ode to Milton on the latter's tercentenary celebration by the British Academy in 1908. Some fragments of even later date survive, showing that Meredith was at work on poetry within weeks of his death. The quantity of his verse was prodigious, although some periods of his life, such as the 1850s and 1880s, seem to have been more productive than others. Within his literary career, Meredith published ten collections of poetry; two more were issued posthumously by his son; and a large amount of verse, partly from his notebooks, partly from his letters, has only recently been collected and published.[1]

Not only in quantity but also in formal and thematic variety does Meredith's poetry equal that of the major Victorian poets. It ranges from brief, simple songs to formal odes and narratives of more than six hundred lines. It contains numerous individual sonnets as well as a cycle of sonnetlike stanzas—"Modern Love." Meredith employs a wide variety of meters, from the common octosyllabic couplet to highly unusual classical meters such as the Galliambic. His poetry includes dramatic monologues, ballads, pastorals, odes, hymns, epitaphs, and translations of parts of *The Iliad* in English hexameter. Its diversity of form and content reveals Meredith's erudition and range of interests as well as his care to find adequate poetic expression for his ideas. As his manuscripts show, he often experimented and revised or discarded; he also used favorite themes and motifs several times in very different shapes.

Much of this material comes across today as flawed or insignificant. It often seems prosy or forced. In many poems, Meredith's style calls attention to itself without rewarding this attention with a fresh insight, and his complex trains of argument in his later poetry are not lightened by melodiousness or easily accessible imagery. But his successful verse still demands attention, not only because Meredith himself wished to be considered primarily a poet, but also because, besides its intellectual challenge, it offers a great deal of genuine aesthetic pleasure. Beyond the autobiographical interest of "Modern Love" and the earnest appeal of his didactic verse, the reader discovers the work of a deliberate artist who combines a traditional system of symbols with a highly idiosyncratic diction in order to explore the relationship of mind with art and nature. At its best Meredith's poetry involves the reader in the actual process of a search to understand man's place in the universe.[2]

Relying almost exclusively on the didactic verse, Trevelyan has called Meredith "the inspired prophet of sanity."[3] This term is too simple for a writer who can evoke the nightmare qualities of sexual passion in his ballads and "Modern Love." But it is true that the quest for a sane mental attitude toward natural and human life is at the heart of Meredith's poetry. The emphasis lies on "quest": many of his poems not only demand but verbally reenact the speaker's search. The idiosyncratic qualities of Meredith's syntax and diction serve to underline the dynamic and suggestive nature of his poetry.

For example, careful reading of a Meredith poem will often correct one's initial impression of "too-muchness."[4] Instead, one may well be struck by the elements of suggestion and concentration. After repeated readings, which Meredith explicitly demanded of his audience (*Letters,* 1:156), much of his apparent garrulousness and obscurity reveals itself in his best verse as necessary for his purpose: to explore the possibility of man's well-being in a world deprived of traditional certainties and transcendent redemption. His stylistic idiosyncrasies support a meliorist worldview inherited from the romantics and adapted to the social conditions and scientific ideas of the later nineteenth century. Although he expresses this worldview also in his personal letters and prose fiction, it comes across most forcefully in his poetry.

The Philosophical Basis

Meredith apparently became an agnostic and evolutionist while a member of Charnock's circle of freethinking, somewhat radical young Londoners from 1846 to 1848. Like many of his educated contemporaries, he could not overlook the findings of biology and paleontology that contradicted orthodox Christianity. He accepted the evolutionist idea that natural history records a continuous development of lower forms of life into higher ones and that every individual is eclipsed by the general progress of the species.[5] Unlike most of his contemporaries, however, Meredith did not regard the obliteration of the individual as a threat to a meaningful existence. Although he concedes that Nature, in her relentless forward march, is not concerned with the single life, he emphasizes that this indifference does not preclude man's happiness on earth. For the person who can fight his way to a proper understanding of his function in the universal scheme, Nature becomes ultimately benign, and Earth, her tangible side, a kind "mother."

Meredith's concern is to point out how men should "read" Earth in order to live productive and joyful lives. Most of his didactic poems are such "readings of life" or "readings of Earth," as the titles of two of his collections suggest. Earth herself presents her meanings in a kind of natural poetry, speaking directly to her devotee, the poet who translates her language. In her "army of unalterable law" ("Lucifer in Starlight," 14), which man needs to observe in order to secure his physical and spiritual well-being, Meredith identifies two supremely important tenets: the inseparableness of life and death, and the need for a balance among "blood," "brain," and "spirit."

In many of his letters Meredith insists that "Death and Life are really one, each to feed the other; and nature has no unkindness for us when we have comprehended this" (*Letters,* 2:911). In his poems he often makes the point in the same abstract terms, or he uses the traditional symbol of organic decay turning into new growth:

> Behold, in yon stripped Autumn, shivering grey,
> Earth knows no desolation.
> She smells regeneration
> In the moist breath of decay.
> ("Ode to the Spirit of Earth in Autumn," 186–89)

To distinguish between life and death is not only spurious but also counterproductive, since it tempts man into either hedonistic self-indulgence or an asceticism—a refusal to love earthly life—that looks toward an illusory afterlife for rewards. The hope for personal immortality distracts us from serving and enjoying this world. Only through understanding that "by Death, as by Life are we fed" ("A Faith on Trial," 421) can we participate in a greater life, which in turn feeds on our individual death:

> Verily now is our season of seed,
> Now in our Autumn; and Earth discerns
> Them that have served her in them that can read,
> Glassing, where under the surface she burns,
> Quick at her wheel, while the fuel, decay,
> Brightens the fire of renewal: and we?
> Death is the word of a bovine day,
> Know you the breast of the springing To-be.
> ("Seed-Time," 6:1–8)

To achieve this insight, Meredith argues, requires long, often harsh courses of natural pedagogy—the "thwackings" Mother Earth administers to her too self-indulgent pupils. Since freedom from egoism can be attained only through ordeals of experience, Meredith's voices are those of adults who have won a glimpse of their position in nature. Like Wordsworth, Meredith ascribes a natural wisdom to the less sophisticated classes whom life has early trained to curb selfish wants; he does not, however, claim this wisdom for children—

voices of children are absent in his poetry. Whatever wisdom we gain, he asserts, must be rooted not in the "glory and the dream" of Wordsworth's "Intimations" ode but in the experience of mundane life: "For the road to her soul is the Real: / The root of the growth of man" ("A Faith on Trial," 391–92).

This emphasis on the "real" does not mean that Meredith places little value on the spiritual. In fact, he argues that man, while part of the physical world, is Nature's glory because he, alone of all her creatures, can perceive, articulate, and celebrate her spiritual side. But man can fulfill his promise only when he maintains a careful balance among "blood," "brain," and "spirit." This law, stated explicitly in "The Woods of Westermain," underlies Meredith's social criticism as well as his psychological ideas:

> Each of each in sequent birth,
> Blood and brain and spirit, three
> (Say the deepest gnomes of Earth),
> Join for true felicity.
> Are they parted, then expect
> Someone sailing will be wrecked.
>   (4:169–74)

Disregarding "Blood" or instinct, man invites the reassertion of repressed desires and fears in disastrous forms; disregarding "Brain" or intellect, he allows selfish goals to limit and confuse his life. The imbalance of instinct and intellect results in a loss of "Spirit," affecting nations and individuals alike. "Spirit" is man's capacity to aspire to beauty and goodness and to perceive a divinity in the very essence of physical Nature. It is thus essential for achieving the integrated vision of life held by the poet.

Of the earlier poets whom Meredith acknowledges as his masters, he wrote to Augustus Jessopp, an Anglican clergyman,

The men to whom I bow my head (Shakespeare; Göthe [sic]; and in their way, Molière, Cervantes) are Realists au fond. . . . They give us Earth; but it is Earth with an atmosphere. (Letters, 1:160–61)

It is this "atmosphere" that suggests the inherent spirituality of Earth and therefore of even her least significant creatures. Meredith's successful poems focus intensely on natural phenomena—a tree, a sky-

lark, a southwestern storm—but not on them alone or for their own
sake. These objects are at the same time vividly real and deeply symbolic; they are part of a mythological system, which also includes
classical divinities and legendary characters and draws heavily on the
pastoral and georgic conventions. This system constantly blurs the
boundaries between the physical and the spiritual, the factual and
the metaphoric. As Meredith asserts in his letter to Jessopp: "Between realism and idealism, there is no natural conflict. This com-
pletes that." Or as his poem "Meditation under Stars" concludes:
"Half strange seems Earth, and sweeter than her flowers."

In his best poems this fusion and transformation come across to the
reader with the unforced simplicity of great art; in a far larger number, one notices Meredith's straining, verbally and syntactically, to
forge the link. The first group—brief stanzas like "Dirge in Woods"
or "Song in the Songless," which occur intermittently throughout his
career—touches the reader immediately, quite apart from their philosophical underpinning; the second, while less satisfying esthetically,
gives us perhaps more insight into Meredith's concern with the purpose and the tools of his art.

"Readings" of Life and Earth

Meredith's first volume of poetry, simply called *Poems* (1851), gives
little indication of his later originality in outlook or tone. It contains
a great number of conventionally pretty occasional pieces and love
songs, sounding somewhat like Herrick or the young Tennyson; a series of dactylic four-liners on the English poets Meredith admired—
Chaucer, Spenser, Shakespeare, Milton, Coleridge, Shelley, Wordsworth, Keats, and, surprisingly, Southey—whose individual voices he
tries to capture in the metaphor of landscapes drawn from their own
poetry; some narratives of classical myth, notable mainly for their
Keatsian lushness; and the first version of "Love in the Valley."

This poem, which employs an unusually lilting measure, shows
Meredith's ability to enter into the spirit of the classical pastoral. The
persona, a young peasant or shepherd, voices his love for a young girl
whose beauty and chastity both delight him. He is obviously eager
for marriage, but the youth of his beloved restrains him. With the
wisdom of those who closely observe Nature he awaits the right time.
The poem is charged with images of sexuality and fertility; psychological tensions hide beneath the surface. But the overall structure of

the poem holds out the promise of release: it traces the progress of
the courtship within the framework of seasonal change. As the year
advances, bringing flowers to fruit and fruit to ripeness, so does the
girl's maturity advance. Unlike the Renaissance sonnet cycles, where
Nature serves only as the canvas on which the poet draws the superior
beauty of his lady, Meredith gives natural objects an exemplary value;
they obey the demands of the season, as man should do also:

> Clambering roses peep into her chamber,
> Jasmine and woodbine breathe sweet, sweet,
> White-necked swallows twittering of summer,
> Fill her with balm and nested peace from head to feet.
> Ah! will the rose-bough see her lying lonely,
> When the petals fall and fierce bloom is on the leaves?
> Will the Autumn garners see her still ungathered,
> When the fickle swallows forsake the weeping eaves?
>   (33–40)

"Love in the Valley" was much changed and expanded by Meredith
for inclusion in his third volume of poetry, *Poems and Lyrics of the Joy
of Earth* (1883). By this time he was trying to suppress the 1851
Poems, calling it his "boy's book" (*Letters,* 1:110). He had become
much more committed to evolutionism and more philosophical in his
poetry, and the new version of "Love in the Valley" shows a distinct
tendency away from the naive fears and hopes of the lover (for example, his worry about potential upper-class rivals) and toward sophisticated reflections, expressed in abstract terms and complex imagery:

> Large and smoky red the sun's cold disk drops,
> Clipped by naked hills, on violet shaded snow:
> Eastward large and still lights up a bower of moonrise,
> Whence at her leisure steps the moon aglow.
> Nightlong on black print-branches our beech-tree
> Gazes in this whiteness: nightlong could I.
> Here may life on death or death on life be painted.
> Let me clasp her soul to know she cannot die.
>   (161–69)

Meredith's second collection, *Modern Love and Poems of the English
Roadside, with Poems and Ballads* (1862), contains not only his most
famous work, "Modern Love," which requires separate discussion, but

also a number of soliloquies by "roadside philosophers"—simple characters such as "Juggling Jerry," who bids his wife a cheerful farewell, awaiting death after a lifetime of juggling, and "the old chartist," who finds an inspiring self-respect in a water rat, which helps him overcome his hostility toward bourgeois society. Although the characters' situations and levels of awareness vary, they function as mouthpieces for Meredith's hardy optimism. The poems have the relaxed, somewhat rambling tone of Browning's dramatic monologues, but little of their tension and irony. In Meredith's later collections the relaxed tone largely disappears, although it surfaces occasionally in some very late verses, where it clashes oddly with his more customary knottiness of style ("The Empty Purse," "The Enamoured Sage").

Meredith's ballads, in this as well as a later collection (*Ballads and Poems of Tragic Life*, 1887), show the poet from a different side, which has elicited recent critical interest: preoccupied with the tragic results of unrestrained human passion, particularly sexual passion.[6] The ballads, small in number and seldom conforming to strict balladic form, deal with the forces of jealousy, pride, suspicion, revenge, and the conflict between uxoriousness and loyalty to one's followers. Dramatizing brief, suggestive incidents, they capture the tragic essence of a human relationship gone awry and, sometimes, the rottenness of an entire culture. In addition, they point to the precariousness of human communication and to the unreliability of appearances—topics Meredith explores at greater length and with more complexity in "Modern Love" and in his novels. The ballads make use of exotic settings, for example, Provence and the camp of Attila the Hun, and employ an archaic, sometimes terse, sometimes overwrought language. True to balladic tradition, Meredith leaves much of their plots inexplicable and weird; the reader is left wondering what Margaret actually tells her fiancé in "Margaret's Bridal Eve" or what actually transpired in the wedding chamber of Attila ("The Nuptials of Attila"). The inexplicable events serve to underline the idea that human life is subject to powerful, uncontrollable forces moving according to their own logic. This idea is not prominent in Meredith's worldview; in fact, his major poems throughout his life project an Apollonian spirit of rational control and balance.

As its title indicates, *Poems and Lyrics of the Joy of Life* (1883) celebrates earthly life; it resonates with energy and zest. This volume contains some of Meredith's most important odes, sonnets, and other reflective poems. He speaks with forcefulness and conviction about

Nature's laws, the community of all living beings, and the poet's role in promoting this community through his unifying vision. In some of his verse urgency leads to prolixity, and his desire to suggest the vast network of connections and possibilities in life may burden his statements with long chains of metaphors. The sonnet form sets a limit to such tendencies, although here Meredith's ellipsis and contorted syntax are often particularly marked. Throughout the volume Meredith requires the reader to be alert and actively involved in the creative process, to supply connective words such as *like, as,* or *and*—with the understanding that these words may circumscribe and limit what Meredith would like to keep open-ended—and to accept the transformations of nouns into verbs, adjectives into nouns, and nouns into adjectives. Such transformations emphasize qualities and processes rather than objects and activities; they help suggest that individual properties and acts somehow reflect the essence of Nature as a whole, particularly her energy and mutability.

"**The Woods of Westermain.**"   The first poem in the 1883 volume and one particularly representative of Meredith's adult philosophy and technique is "The Woods of Westermain." Its invitation to "enter these enchanted woods, / You who dare" (1–2) pertains both to the reading of Meredith's poetry and to the entry into a magical world. It asks the reader to look unflinchingly at human and natural life as presented in all its potentialities.

The voice of the speaker is gnomic, with an incantatory quality supported by the trochaic tetrameter, an unusual meter in English verse. But it would oversimplify the poem to read it as a mere string of didactic statements, such as the famous "Blood and brain and spirit, three . . . / Join for true felicity" (4:170–72). The verses themselves imitate the walk through the woods of Westermain, and their difficulties provide a testing ground of their own.[7] The walk carries not only the promise of a sane enchantment through innumerable visual and aural pleasures but also the risk of terror and nightmare. The poem alternates between promise and warning, but underneath this seemingly firm structure, the linguistic ground, like the geographic one, is constantly shifting, throwing the reader off balance. Most important, the poem appears to present the phenomena of the forest as disparate and fragmented, while a careful reading discloses the interconnectedness of the images. They form a network of associations made more complex from stanza to stanza: birds, for example, serve at first simply as natural objects in a natural forest, (2:5–8), then as images of sensuous delight (3:17–22) and as a metaphor for poetry (3:30–32), and finally as an image for the heavenward soaring of wisdom (4:21–29). But imaged in the owl and the vulture are also potential horrors.

For the traveler who enters the woods, Nature offers delight progressing from simple sensory pleasures through a perception of harmony and love to the wisdom that accepts change as the law of life. But this progress is promised only to a person who "loves light so well / "That no darkness will seem fell" (4:1–2). Those who fear and distrust Nature, particularly those who have assumed the "proud title of elect" and cherished the dragon of Self, undergo nightmares of alienation and despair. In a mystical vision the traveler is led to the fountain of life, where beginning and end are the same, and is shown that his own spirit is but a part of a greater one. If he has the right understanding of earth, he will strive for a balance of blood, brain, and spirit, because earth herself embodies this balance, and will serve her fearlessly and unselfishly. But Meredith does not end with this apotheosis of man as part of the universal spirit. Insight is, after all, conditional on will and patience. Therefore, the last section of the poem reverses the earlier mystical images, turning them into a vision of hideousness and decay: the distortions of beauty, love, and wisdom when governed by egoism. And egoism is abetted by man's desire to see a clear, distinct goal in the world's movement—an unequivocal Eden. Meredith considers such a hope self-contradictory. The walk through the woods of Westermain does not and must not end. Therefore, the verses conclude with a return to the beginning: the initial warning is now charged with the full resonance of the entire poem's potentialities.

The language of "The Woods of Westermain" is densely allusive. Since the poem's scope is so vast—ranging from the right relationship between the sexes (3:97–140) to the evolution of man from the lower animals (3:45–49)—it needs a vocabulary and syntax able to compress and connect large areas of human experience. Meredith condenses through omnibus metaphors, in which he heaps image upon image. For example, he first compares life to a tidal world, and then to a field of windy wheat, which may be either "momently black, barren, rude" or "golden-brown, for harvest meet" but also "dragon-reaped from folly-sown" or "bride-like to the sickle-blade" (4:233–38). Such shifting metaphors require the reader's constant attention. The same holds true for Meredith's use of ellipsis, which in this poem not only supports the tone of magic but also suggests a multiplicity of possible meanings. To get the point of this incantation, the reader must keep in mind that two different kinds of "woods" are invoked. Both of them are equally possible and equally "real" in the poet's imagination, but their existence is contingent on the reader's own attitude. Thus the poem invites us to explore the landscape of the mind and moves us toward creating for ourselves the kind of "woods" that most reflect our sense of freedom and fulfillment. The message of "The Woods of Westermain" does not affirm the existence of an idyllic Eden in human experience; it does affirm man's ability to mold human experience through steadfast and courageous vision. With this theme the poem fittingly introduces a collection of verse that confidently places the imagination at the center of spiritual and natural life.

Following directly on "The Woods of Westermain," two other remarkable poems focus on the transforming power of the mind's eye, specifically that of the poet. Both of them illustrate Meredith's tendency to clothe his insights in narrative; one, "A Ballad of Past Meridian," combines a speaker's "personal" account with allegory; the other, "The Day of the Daughter of Hades," tells a myth of Meredith's own invention. In both of them, man encounters mythical figures who pronounce enduring truths; man listens, registers, and records these truths in song. The narrative strategy has the effect of distancing. It eliminates emphasis on the poet's self, precluding an impression of egocentricity. It also allows for the play of several different perspectives as well as tension and resolution.

"A Ballad of Past Meridian." In "A Ballad of Past Meridian," a short poem of three five-line stanzas, the persona first meets Death, "the grey mist." Upon receiving Death's wilted flowers, he laments the "bitterness" of this nosegay, but Death only answers, "I gather." In contrast to the formlessness of Death, Life, whom the speaker encounters next, is a shape of harsh outlines: "Sword-hacked and iron-stained, with breasts of clay, / And metal veins that sometimes fiery shone." Life's response to the speaker's outcry of dismay is: "As thou hast carved me, such am I." Faced with the bitterness of Death and the hardness of Life, the persona is sustained by memory and hope:

> Then memory, like the nightjar on the pine,
> And sightless hope, a woodlark in night sky,
> Joined notes of Death and Life till night's decline:
> Of Death, of Life, those inwound notes are mine.
>
> (12–15)

The poem's pattern is a simple contrast, followed by a more complex resolution. In the third stanza the allegorical figures are transformed into objects of human thought—notes of the song composed out of memory and hope—and as the tense switch from past to present in the last line makes clear, the poem itself is the result of the synthesizing poetic perception: life and death are joined, "inwound" in it. The singing sustains man through the dark night of spiritual desolation. Such a vision does not sentimentalize human experience; Meredith does not provide a facile answer to the harshness of life or to the absoluteness of death. The persona's laments, placed prominently in the last lines of stanzas 1 and 2, get only the bleakest responses from the allegorical figures. Yet Life's answer, holding man accountable for the shape of his course on earth, also points to his inner resources for structuring and interpreting his destiny; the "Then" of line 12 indicates not only a temporal but also a causal sequence.

Because of its skillful modulating of allegory into symbolism, along with the economy of its imagery and language, "A Ballad of Past Meridian" is one of Meredith's most successful reflective poems. He uses the allegorical figures of Life and Death several other times, most notably in "Hymn to Color," in which Color, apostrophized by Love, takes the place of memory and hope. This poem is overburdened by the multiplicity of allegorical figures and abstractions, and it does not work out any contrast between Life and Death, who remain shady half-personifications. Love, in fact, asserts that they are one, but the poem itself does not demonstrate this identity.

In addition to allegorical figures, Meredith frequently uses stories and characters of Greek mythology to express his ideas. Among them Apollo and Demeter are most prominent: Demeter, because she embodies earthly fertility and the comedy arising from an unsentimental appreciation of Nature ("The Appeasement of Demeter"); Apollo, because as the god of light and poetry he symbolizes the progress of human civilization—an advancement possible only through a clear-eyed, sober view of the human condition ("The Day of the Daughter of Hades," "Phoebus with Admetus," "Melampus").

"The Day of the Daughter of Hades." Like the "Ballad of Past Meridian," "The Day of the Daughter of Hades" dramatizes the rise of poetry through a unified vision of life and death and employs narrative both to frame and to mimic the theme's progress. In its stylistic features—archaic diction, convoluted syntax, and unusual, often cumulative imagery—it is representative of much of Meredith's longer poetry, and its subject throws additional light on the poet's conception of his art.

Meredith's invented myth of the meeting between Callistes, a Sicilian youth, and Skiageneia ("Born of a Shade"), the daughter of Pluto and Proserpina, continues the classical Proserpina myth. According to legend, Pluto abducted Proserpina, the daughter of Demeter, goddess of vegetation and fertility, from the field of Enna in Sicily, but allowed her to visit her mother one day every spring; from this meeting comes earth's annual renewal. Over the years Proserpina herself became a symbol of death so that the meeting between her and Demeter could be seen as a meeting of life and death. Meredith is not concerned with this part of the myth and sketches it only briefly. But when Callistes comes to the field of Enna to watch a spring sunrise, he not only witnesses the encounter between mother and daughter but also meets the granddaughter, Skiageneia, who has slipped out of Hades in irrepressible longing for the light of day. The poem recounts how Callistes accompanies her on her one day in the world, falls in love with her, listens to her song, relinquishes her at the end of the day, and lives on, devastated but transformed into a true poet by this encounter.

From the outset the poem is concerned with the quality of vision; as a prefatory stanza warns, the "marvellous tale" will remain just that, a story out of classical mythology, unless the reader himself is able to look on Earth "deeper than flower and fruit," the emblems of life—unless he is, in effect, also a Callistes. But Callistes becomes a true poet only through his love for Skiageneia. Thus the poem concentrates on her. It follows her as she rambles through the fields, ascends a mountain, and obeying the order from Pluto, descends again to the underworld. The plot is very simple; as usual with Meredith, what actually happens matters little. Time, on the other hand, figures prominently, both chronologically and psychologically. It provides the organizing framework for Skiageneia's holiday; the sun's ascent and descent mirror her own. The passage of time is continuously in her mind, giving poignancy to her experience. How to conquer time while acknowledging its invincible power—this is the paradoxical problem the poem poses.

As a goddess, Skiageneia should not be subject to the effects of change. But Meredith's mythical figures are often not so much superhuman as exemplary in their insight into a fate that affects them as much as it does the rest of nature. As the daughter of death, with a yearning for light and life, Skiageneia is an image of man, while her intensity of feeling and depth of vision mark her as the ideal poet. As a whole, the poem thus offers its own solution to the problem of mutability: the creative activity of the poet.

Walking through the countryside, Skiageneia names the natural objects she encounters:

> She smiled,
> Recounting again and again
> Corn, wine, fruit, oil! like a child,
> With the meaning known to men.
> (6:53–56)

On the mountain summit her words crystallize into a hymn to Apollo, god of light and god of poetry. But this song grows out of common human experience; it is "but a Song of Days / Where the husbandman's toil and strife / Little varies to strife and toil" (8:57–58). In its characteristic Meredithian identification of poetry and daylight ("Song of Days"), this song points out the creative power of the imagination in dealing with the most mundane material. Naming an object has traditionally been associated with magic: what is named is called into existence. In other poems, such as "Earth and Man" of the same 1883 volume, Meredith asserts that man and earth share a love for the shaped and distinctly realized; they both shun the formless. Yet since flux is one of the unalterable laws of the universe, the ideal poet calls the object into existence only with the intense awareness of its temporary nature, and only through the love that is heightened by this awareness. Skiageneia knows this; Callistes learns it, not only by listening to her song, but also by losing her—a fact that transforms his life as well as his poetry. The narrative depicts him as pining away for his beloved. There is thus a warning in his story that for all its celebratory, creative work the poetic impulse runs true only when charged with a sense of transitoriness. It is a burden as much as a gift.

In spite of the poignancy of this message, "The Day of the Daughter of Hades" conveys an impression of tremendous energy and "joy of earth," in accordance with the title of Meredith's volume of 1883. Of the large number of poems sharing this spirit, two others in which Meredith adapts Greek mythology are notable.

"Phoebus with Admetus" celebrates the glory of the days when the god Phoebus Apollo resided among men on earth:

> God! of whom music
> And song and blood are pure,
> The day is never darkened
> That had thee here obscure.
>   (1:9–12)

The speaker, a simple farmer, marvels at the fertility of earth under Apollo's careful, intelligent husbandry. The poem makes clear that this abundance has nothing to do with magic; the divine model of Apollo simply calls out the best efforts in his human fellow workers. And not only nature's abundance but also poetry, music, wisdom, and love result from the communal labor of men and god. Thus the poem traces the growth of civilization out of service, intelligence, and respect for earth—qualities exemplified by Apollo and increasingly shared by his "housemates," the human workers. This growth is the evolution Meredith envisions and hopes to foster through his poetry. In the new gospel of his philosophy, in which Apollo takes on a Christ-like role of god-man, man's redemption is not deferred until the afterlife, and his brotherhood with divinity does not come about through supernatural grace, but through his innate strength calling him to excellence in his work.

Apollo's teachings again figure prominently in "Melampus," which narrates another classical myth. The "good physician" Melampus observes and loves all creatures of earth. In gratitude for his protection, a brood of snakes licks his ears while he is asleep. This act gives him the ability to understand the language of wildlife, and he pursues, with heightened wisdom and reverence, the mysteries of life. As a reward for his service, Apollo shows him the ties between art and nature and teaches him that poetry derives all its force from a faithful love of earth:

> And there vitality, there, there solely in song,
> Resides, where earth and her uses to men, their needs,
> Their forceful cravings, the theme are: there is it strong,
> The Master said. . . .
>   (14:1–4)

Melampus does not turn poet, but it is clear from Apollo's words that Meredith sees the same capacity for healing both in the true physician and in the true poet: both of them bring sanity and order to their fellowmen through their "love exceeding a simple love of the things / That glide in grasses and rubble of woody wreck" (1-2).

Poems claiming that poetry arises from a careful, loving observation of nature, as Meredith's do, must themselves show evidence of this observation without falling into the drab naturalism or the sentimental prettifying Meredith deplored in much of contemporary literature. Through highly idiosyncratic diction and syntax, the poet tries to suggest in the patter of a small animal the forward march of universal evolution. His style is marked, first of all, by a strong attention to detail.[8] Visitors to Box Hill have left testimony of Meredith's excellent eye for wildlife and his wide knowledge of natural lore; the poems confirm this interest by their specificity and precision. Sounds are rendered onomatopoeically: "Chirrup, drone, bleat, and buzz ringed the lake" ("Day of the Daughter of Hades," 6:32); colors are defined and redefined: "the young bronze-orange leaf" (6:35), "To the groves of olive grey, / Downy-grey, golden-tinged" (6:46–47); movement—and there is always movement in Meredith's descriptions—is conveyed with precise verbs: "Where ripple ripple overcurls / And eddy into eddy whirls" ("Lark Ascending," 7–8). Although the setting may be idyllically beautiful, Meredith stresses the slightly irregular and offbeat; he takes particular note of twisted trees, off-key music, and other unexpected details. In many verses, sequences of modifiers suggest an ongoing refining and refocusing of the poet's vision in order to pinpoint a quality or process as exactly as possible. Compound words—many of Meredith's own making—and series of nouns, verbs, or adjectives without connective words convey not so much an impression of accomplished precision as the speaker's urgency to get closer and closer to the essence of his object. In its redefining and modulating, Meredith's language reflects the expansion of poetic vision along with the sharpening of focus. These stylistic features are common, more or less, to all his poems of the 1880s, but they are exceptionally striking in "The Lark Ascending."

"The Lark Ascending." Among poetic birds of the nineteenth century, the skylark figures prominently, particularly for the romantics. Its habit of quickly rising straight into the air, often as early as sunrise—which has led to its traditional association with light and rebirth—and its apparently effortless singing while suspended invisi-

bly between heaven and earth have made it a symbol of joy, spirituality, and poetry. Meredith wrote two skylark poems; the first one, "To
a Skylark," (1851), echoes both Shelley and Wordsworth, showing
unmistakably his roots in the romantic tradition:

> O skylark! I see thee and call thee joy!
> . . . .
> Thus are the days when I was a boy;
> Sweet while I lived in them, dear now they're gone;
> I feel them no longer, but still, O still
> They tell of the heavens to me.
>
> (1:1, 5–8)

The mature Meredith rejects the sentimental evocation of childhood
memories as well as the trite spiritualizing of the bird. In "The Lark
Ascending" the bird is still "joy," but a joy radiating from the object
itself and not superimposed on it by the poet's enthusiasm. The poem
sets itself the task of revealing earth's spirituality without distortion
by the poet's "taint of personality " (94). At the same time it defines
the poetic process as a precarious balancing between a detached perception of its object and a complete fusion of perceiver and perceived.
The fragility of this position distinguishes Meredith from Shelley and
Wordsworth and provides some interesting paradoxes in the poem.
"The Lark Ascending" is a verbal tour de force, simultaneously de-
scribing the skylark's ascent, reproducing its flight song, and conveying a typical Meredithian message of the glory of natural life.

Ostensibly the subject matter is the physical rise of the bird into
the sky, observed by a detached persona. But as even the first stanza
makes clear by its constant onomatopoeia, it is the song that arrests
the observer, and the song is its own message. While the reader, following the stanza's "silver chain of sound" on its own spiral progress,
traces the bird's upward movement, he himself is led from physical
observation to spiritual contemplation. The real subject of "The Lark
Ascending" is, as it was for Shelley's poem, the poetic imagination.
But Meredith stresses, through the onomatopoeia, the spiral structure
and the message itself, that poetry always and only gives form to what
is already inherent as a potential poem in nature. The skylark, poet
par excellence like Skiageneia, is stimulated to song by the sun's light
and its own pleasure in being. It does what Nature means it to do;
the quintessence of the poem's message is that human song arises out

of the same impulse. To reach this insight—the fundamental identity of "being" and "singing"—involves a widening of perspective, just as the lark has a larger view from its greater height:

> The woods and brooks, the sheep and kine,
> He is, the hills, the human line,
> The meadows green, the fallows brown,
> The dreams of labor in the town;
> He sings the sap, the quickened veins;
> The wedding song of suns and rains
> He is . . .
>
> (71–77)

Not only have the skylark's being and song fused in the speaker's imagination ("He is," "He sings," "The wedding song . . . he is"), but the bird has also become the elements of earthly life on which, according to Meredith, man's well-being rests.

The poem moves from the initial identification of bird and speaker, by way of the verbal reenactment of flight and song, to a temporary differentiation when the speaker contrasts the bird's healthy attitude with human weakness of spirit: "Our wisdom speaks from failing blood, / Our passion is too full in flood" (89–90), echoing the statement of "Woods of Westermain" that blood and brain must be well balanced for psychological health. But Meredith cannot stop with this contrast between bird and speaker; it would contradict the logic of the poem. While men may never be such perfect singers as the skylark (or Skiageneia), their own efforts to serve life and their love for earth "yield substance sweet for song." Such men are part of the poem of earth, thus also part of the bird's song and part of the poet's imagination, which, in itself, "through self-forgetfulness divine" is part of the universal song embodied by the bird. Toward the end the references to bird, men, and poet become increasingly difficult to unravel. Finally, when we lose track of the lark both visually and aurally, Meredith makes the fusion between its song and the poet's imagination explicit. But it is, after all, only a potential fusion at the border of discourse as well as the border of heaven, and it silences both the poetic voice and the poetic object.

A Reading of Earth.   For all its complexity of structure and shifts of focus, the spirit of "The Lark Ascending" is simply celebratory. Meredith's confidence in the goodness of life gives this poem, as well as the other pieces in *Poems and Lyrics of the Joy of Earth,* an extraordinary buoyancy of tone. In the collection *A Reading of Earth* (1888), he adopts a more subdued voice. The volume is marked by the personal ordeal he suffered when his wife died after a long, courageous struggle with cancer. Some of the poems show evidence of a "faith on trial" trying to reconcile itself to the apparent heartlessness of Nature and to find in the ever-returning beauty of the seasons a guarantee of a benevolent Master Spirit. Meredith saw personal despair as a sign of unenlightened egoism and his struggle against it as part of the common labor in the cause of evolution. His imagery at this period and further on is characterized by metaphors of unending battle: "Wisdom is won of its fight, / The combat incessant" ("A Faith on Trial," 469–70). The endlessness of the endeavor in itself bears witness to the reality of evolution, and the struggle refines and ennobles the human spirit in his individual growth.

The tension inherent in this worldview appears even in "Dirge in Woods," one of the few poems in which Meredith refrains entirely from didacticism. Perhaps because the occasion for writing this poem was the death of his father-in-law, an old man, after a full and satisfying life, the poet was able to assume a calm, detached view. The brevity of the lines in the single stanza, the sparseness of descriptive words, the unobtrusiveness of its first three similes—these all contribute to a general impression of reticence and supreme poetic control. As a result, "Dirge in Woods" has been praised as "pure poetry," like Goethe's "Wanderer's Nachtlied," with which it has indeed some affinities both in outlook and language.[9] But despite Meredith's reserve, his poem shows a much greater complexity than Goethe's, necessitated by the contrasts between "below" and "overhead," life and death, which the poem seeks to harmonize:

> A wind sways the pines,
> And below,
> Not a breath of wild air;
> Still as the mosses that glow
> On the flooring and over the lines
> Of the roots here and there.
> The pine-tree drops its dead;
> They are quiet, as under the sea.
> Overhead, overhead
> Rushes life in a race,
> As the clouds the clouds chase;

And we go,
And we drop like the fruits of the tree,
Even we,
Even so.

(1–15)

"Dirge in Woods" moves from the depiction of a natural scene to a metaphor about human life. In the descriptive first six lines its focus appears blurred; we barely register that the mosses and roots are part of a comparison the object of which remains hidden. In line 7 the metaphor of "its dead" prepares for a transition from the natural to the human, but this movement is retarded by emphasis on quietude and the contrasting "overhead," which appear to keep the following lines on the level of natural description. Only in line 9, with "Rushes life in a race," does the transition to a philosophical statement become obvious: the moving clouds now figure as an image of life. From this shift in perspective the last four lines follow inevitably; if the wind swaying the pines can be equated with life, pine seeds can be equated with the human dead and, conversely, the human dead with pine seeds. Thus human transience is part of the same large process that makes the tree quietly release its fruit. In retrospect the blurred focus of lines 1–6 shows itself as right for a poem dealing with life and death rather than the airy disturbance of pine trees. Equally appropriate, however, is the onomatopoeic force in the last lines, mirroring not only the quietude of the "below" but also the "drop" of the fruit, and thus placing man, as concretely as a poem can, in the natural scheme of things.

The "pine-tree fruit" metaphor is, of course, conventional. So is the image of life as a rushing wind. Meredith may have adopted both from Shelley's "Ode to the West Wind." What makes "Dirge in Woods" a particularly successful poem is the way in which metaphor and content coalesce. While it starts with a natural scene as an image for the human condition, it ends, in effect, with the human condition as a metaphor for Nature. In such a reading of Earth the poet seems to step back and let the subject speak for itself.

With an acute eye for contrast Meredith juxtaposed "Dirge in Woods" with the next poem in the collection, "A Faith on Trial." It is one of his longest poems and his most personal one; autobiographical references—for instance, to his wife's French background—are frequent and obvious. The work gives an unusually direct glimpse at the

suffering Meredith underwent and traces his struggle to reconcile
himself to it.

It is a May morning; the speaker is out on his customary ramble
through the woods, but although he notices birdsong and swelling
buds, his mind is preoccupied with memories and an overwhelming
sense of loss:

> Alone do we stand, each one,
> Till rootless as they we strew
> Those deeps of the corse-like stare
> At a foreign and stony sun.
>   (101–4)

Only one thing still links him to earth: "My disciplined habit to
see." But this habit brings with it memories of earlier sights. Thus
when he suddenly comes across a white wild cherry in bloom, the impact of the vision has an unexpected force: not only the beauty of the
tree itself but also the memory of his youth, with its dreams, its
wishes, and its unbroken trust in earth, challenge his spiritual dead-
ness. As in "The Ballad of Past Meridian," memory unites with
hope—hope arising out of the mystical beauty of the tree, which calls
up images of angelic hosts: "My Goddess, the chaste, not
chill; / Choir over choir white-robed; / White-bosomed fold within
fold" (282–84). From the sight of the tree and the memories it stirs,
he learns that men can be "chords to the Nature without, / Orbs to
the greater whole" (330–31).

If Meredith had chosen to stop at this point, he would have given
dignified expression to his grief, worked out a psychologically plausi-
ble resolution to it, and suggested, rather than made explicit, the
general validity of his experience. "A Faith on Trial," however, goes
on for another three hundred lines of meditation and evolutionary
philosophy, partly "quoted" from the whispers of Earth the speaker
apparently overhears. These lines constitute, of course, the insight he
had gleaned from his memory-charged vision, but the connection is
soon lost to the reader, despite occasional echoes of the image of the
cherry tree. The poem ranges over a large area of human thought connected with the theme of death, from the role of religion to the birth
of reason out of our contact with reality, from reason's fight against
the "old worm" egoism to the futility of the question "whither." Af-

ter the characteristically Meredithian admonition to work unselfishly and without concern for the future, it ends with an apotheosis of evolutionary idealism as a "dream of the blossom of Good."

The poem's lines—irregularly rhymed trimeters—seem to roll on and on, but on closer examination they show a great deal of repetition behind the stately cadences. In fact, some of Earth's words are verbatim echoes of the speaker's statements, proof that his insight has the approval of the great Mother herself. This device may be logically justified, but it overworks the point Meredith makes. In addition, the second half of the poem employs not only large clusters of telescoped metaphors but also a great many abstract terms. As the poem moves away from the concreteness of the Box Hill woods and the poignant memories linked with them, the force of its statement dissipates into countless vague, disparate images and impressions.

Unfortunately, the flaws of "A Faith on Trial" foreshadow a general decline of Meredith's poetic power in his later years. The volumes after 1890 contain fewer pieces than the earlier ones, and these often very long poems—for example, "The Empty Purse" and "The Sage Enamoured and the Honest Lady"—are marked by abstract vocabulary and repetition. They exaggerate the knotty syntax and complicated imagery already evident in the poetry of his best years. Perhaps his physical ailments are partly to blame for these defects: no longer able to roam over the countryside, Meredith could not draw inspiration directly from Nature as he had before, and his deafness caused him to monopolize conversation, pouring out streams of sentences in often agitated monologue. Also, he had become a recognized national "sage" who was expected to speak out on political and historical matters not amenable to concrete and pithy treatment. In his "Odes in Contribution to the Song of French History" (1898) he analyzes the "genius" of France and its antithetical "genius" Napoleon and points out France's responsibility for losing Alsace-Lorraine. In "The Empty Purse" he admonishes England's wealthy young aristocracy to be less self-indulgent; in "The Sage Enamoured and the Honest Lady" he criticizes society's hypocritical attitude toward sex and women. These poems—heavily didactic, overwrought, and obscure—are difficult to appreciate, although they are sometimes lightened by traces of rueful self-irony and always show a noble, generous, and courageous spirit. Their intellectual and moral toughness is undeniable, but they merely assert what in his earlier years Meredith had been able to evoke through the magic of his more natural song.

"Modern Love"

"Modern Love," published in 1862, consists of fifty individual poems tied together by a recognizable story and an intricate network of symbols. Each poem has sixteen lines in iambic pentameter, the meter traditionally used in the English sonnet. This stanzaic form was invented by Meredith, but used only in "Modern Love," for which it is particularly suited. Lacking the emphatically placed final couplet of the traditional sonnet, the poems suggest open-endedness and avoid the impression of a pat final answer to the dialectics raised in the individual stanzas.[10]

The plot of "Modern Love" is uncomplicated, although at first reading the complexities of language and point of view in each sonnet may be baffling. A husband discovers that his wife has turned from him to a lover, although it is not clear whether the affair has been consummated. Frustrated by jealousy and hurt vanity, he broods over past, present, and future. Society forces the couple to play games of conjugal bliss. The husband takes a mistress, but although this affair is consummated, it does not bring him happiness since it is based chiefly on his desire for revenge. A renewal of sexual intimacy between husband and wife only reveals more devastatingly the death of their old relationship. A brief interlude of open speech seems to promise peace, but this communication leads to misunderstanding: mistaking his affection for mere pity, the wife quietly rejects it and commits suicide in order to release him, as Meredith explained in letters to his friends, to marry the other woman—no longer his intention at all.

"Modern Love" tells a story where "passions spin the plot" and lovers are "betrayed by what is false within" (43:15–16). Meredith wrote the poem during the fall and winter of 1861, shortly after he had heard of the death of Mary Nicolls, his first wife, who had returned sick and unhappy to England after her elopement with Henry Wallis, but whom he had refused to see or help. Under these circumstances the fairness Meredith shows in analyzing the couple's relationship is most remarkable. Although here, as in real life, it was the wife who left the husband, the full weight of our scrutiny falls on the husband, and what his thoughts reveal about himself is not pretty. In the poem, for instance, he initiates an affair to console himself. Nothing of that kind is known of Meredith's own life. On the other hand, Meredith and his wife had a son; he had found her desertion of the

child particularly unnatural. In "Modern Love" no child exists to put
extra blame on the unfaithful woman. And in "Modern Love" the
wife commits suicide from noble motives, whereas Mary Nicolls died
a natural death. Clearly, Meredith was not out to avenge himself in
verse. In the poem he overcame his personal resentment to create a
clear-eyed but also compassionate study of incompatible natures
searching for a reasonable way of living together. Along with the psychological conflicts he also examined the social and biological issues
bearing upon the relationship of a sensitive, well-educated modern
couple—for example, the simple fact of their aging and changing,
which their alienation from nature prevents them from accepting.

The title of the poem leads at once into a crucial problem: is this
"love-match," as he called the work during the earliest stages of conception, intended as a critique and an indictment of the idea of love
as it appears in late nineteenth-century civilization? Meredith's own
brief comment, in a letter to Jessopp in 1862, seems to indicate so,
since he calls "Modern Love" a "dissection of the sentimental passion
of these days" (*Letters,* 1:160). But compared to his novels, the poem
does not show much of the "comic spirit" which normally accompanies Meredith's dissections of sentimentality. Its treatment is not satiric, but ironic—standards of right attitudes and behavior, although
perceivable between the lines, become elusive as soon as they are put
into words by the protagonist, and what the omniscient narrator offers as the last word on the story in sonnet 50 is partly a warning
against too much dissection. "Modern Love" is a "modern" poem because it comments on what Meredith saw as a modern problem: it
calls attention to the varieties and limitations of the ways man struc-
tures and expresses his experiences. Poetic conventions, from the
Renaissance pastoral through Shakespearean tragedy to the nineteenth-
century French novel, figure prominently throughout the poem,
offering models of a coherent vision on life, but breaking down into
disparate clichés under the scrutiny of the suffering protagonist.[11]

The two kinds of sentimentalism involved in "Modern Love" are
the ones discussed earlier in this chapter: the repression of genuine
feelings and the denial of change. The poem demonstrates what "The
Woods of Westermain" asserts—that a blocking of one's passions,
along with an excessive worship of intellect, brings out a "brutish"
side of man. The interior monologues of the husband amply illustrate
this process. On the one hand, they place the protagonists firmly
within their civilization: the couple is upper class, socially active,

well educated. The husband discourses on evolution, *Othello,* gambling, French novels, and Raphael's paintings. Yet these topics inevitably lead him to venting his personal frustration; jealousy, desire, and bafflement break through the slick, elegant rhetoric of the educated gentleman. He is aware of this himself; part of his rage comes from seeing himself morally sinking. In sonnet 33, he discourses on the theme "While mind is mastering clay, gross clay invades it"—an epigram encapsuling the paradox of "Modern Love." The sonnet itself demonstrates the truth of the theme, since it ends with the husband deliberately provoking the wife's jealousy and thus revealing "gross clay"—in the form of mental cruelty.

The couple's resistance to change determines the course of the plot. The two partners have fixed ideas about each other, themselves, and the nature of love. They still try to see themselves, after years of married life, as "lovers beneath the singing sky of May" (50:5)—or rather, they would like to continue seeing themselves this way, but change is irresistible. Their concept of love derives from the Neoplatonic idealism informing the Renaissance sonnet cycles and asserting the eternity of all true love. Their history, on the other hand, demonstrates the paradox that the more one insists on love's unchangeability, the more it changes. "Cravings for the buried day" offer no help for the couple's present life; in fact, sentimental reminiscences, combined with anger at the present, also taint the past in retrospect (sonnet 12). Blotting out the past, as both partners try to do in their affairs, only leads to greater disillusionment, because partly—they find out—the Renaissance poets are right: love is eternal, but it must change, "feeding" on the advancing hours (sonnet 50).

"Modern Love," then, is chiefly a record of the husband's struggle to accept the necessity of change. In the course of this struggle he has to disillusion himself not only about the permanence of happiness but also about his belief that he is a refined and exceptionally deserving specimen of manhood. His progress is traceable through his interior monologues; it is real, but does not advance enough to carry the wife along into a new, satisfactory relationship, and until the very end is marred by misunderstandings of himself and her. Therefore the concluding lines of the speaker in sonnet 50 make no mention of his progress but focus entirely on the tragedy of failed readings of life that have marked the couple's relationship.

The presence of two perspectives in "Modern Love"—the omniscient third-person narrator, who tells the story in the past tense, and the husband, who lives through or relives the events in the present tense—poses a problem for the reader. There is a clear shift from narrator to husband after sonnet 9 and back to the narrator for the last two sonnets. But within each of the first nine poems, objective narrative modulates into interior monologue; the narrator seems to slip into the husband's mind. The fact that he almost never enters the wife's thoughts gives credence to the possibility that Meredith meant the narrator and husband to be identical.[12] In this view a bereaved husband looks back on his failed marriage, trying to analyze it objectively—hence using the third-person, past-tense voice at the beginning and end of the poem—and breaking, again and again, into emotions not recollected in tranquillity. This pattern would, of course, correspond to what we assume was Meredith's own situation. It might be argued, on the other hand, that the philosophical statements sprinkled through the poem, particularly in sonnets 13 and 30 as well as the conclusion, reflect Meredith the sage rather than the husband. Yet most of these comments are qualified by the dramatic context; the husband seems to say, in effect, that he knows theoretically the "lesson of our only visible friend," Nature, but does not feel supported by it because he is not a "scientific animal." The detached wisdom of the conclusion is prepared for by the preceding sonnet's end: "And he knew all." Perhaps the bereaved husband, who looks back on the entire tragedy, has grown through this retrospective examination to a conclusion about life, as the husband within the tragedy has recognized the nature of his wife at the end. But partly because of the difference in perspective between the first nine and the last two sonnets, partly because of the self-directed irony in sonnet 50 ("Ah, what a dusty answer gets the soul / When hot for certainties in this our life!" 11–12), the exact relationship between narrator and husband remains ambiguous.[13]

The main impact of the poem on the reader derives from the subtle tracing of the couple's relationship through the husband's eyes. The story also traces the husband's attempts at self-knowledge; a response to the disaster of his marriage, these attempts simultaneously contribute to it because they project a series of false personae to whom the wife responds. Through various kinds of posturing the husband tries to assuage his pride and to maintain psychological control over his life. Yet, as the sonnets demonstrate, control is spurious as long as it rests on an unceasing fascinated stare at an object—his wife—that refuses to be pinned down in simple terms. In the end, the husband comes to some authenticity of feeling—pity and respect for her, regret for wasted years—but by then it is too late for her to understand

these emotions as genuine. Adding to the complexity of this relationship, and therefore to the subtlety of point of view, is the husband's
at least partial awareness of his false positions, an awareness making
him often as ironic about himself as about the whole situation.

An example of his self-conscious posturing is found in sonnet 15.
Here he sees himself as a latter-day Othello, half-congratulating himself on his magnanimity, half-frustrated by his lack of plain brutality.
He shows a mean streak of sadism along with the theatricality of his
language:

> I think she sleeps: it must be sleep, when low
> Hangs that abandoned arm toward the floor;
> The face turned with it. Now make fast the door.
> Sleep on: it is your husband, not your foe.
> The Poet's black stage-lion of wronged love
> Frights not our modern dames:—well if he did!
> Now will I pour new light upon that lid,
> Full-sloping like the breasts beneath. 'Sweet dove,
> Your sleep is pure. Nay, pardon: I disturb.
> I do not? good!' Her waking infant stare
> Grows woman to the burden my hands bear:
> Her own handwriting to me when no curb
> Was left on Passion's tongue. She trembles through;
> A woman's tremble—the whole instrument:—
> I show another letter lately sent.
> The words are very like: the name is new.

This sonnet, with its melodramatic suspense, the ironic citation
from *Othello* modulating into a sarcastic parody of social tone, and the
almost clinically detached description of her awakening, is impressive
enough in itself. But it receives, as all the sonnets do, a particular
effect from its place in the poem. In sonnet 14 the husband thinks
he can detect jealousy in the wife, that despite her unfaithfulness she
may still love him: "Such love I prize not, madam: by your
leave, / The game you play at is not to my mind." Sonnet 15, then,
ironically comments on the one before, since the husband himself is
quite obviously jealous, and his game is more sadistic than hers. His
self-righteousness in sonnet 14 is undercut by his posturing as
Othello manqué. In sonnet 16, he looks back on happier times, suggesting that in their "old shipwrecked days" their games were less
questionable—although he also comments ironically on his own
youthful posturing. The theme of game playing is carried through to

sonnet 17, a brilliant description of the couple's clever performance as hosts at a party, and contrasted with the ostensibly honest relationship of "Jack and Tom . . . paired with Moll and Meg" at a country merrymaking:

> Heaven keep them happy! Nature they seem near.
> They must, I think, be wiser than I am;
> They have the secret of the bull and lamb.
> 'Tis true that when we trace its source, 'tis beer.
>
> (sonnet 18)

The last line cynically invalidates the Arcadian idyll and, as the following sonnet makes clear, implies a rejection of all easy solutions: "No state is enviable" except, he concludes, that of the idiot.

As a glance at these few poems illustrates, the various parts of "Modern Love" are linked by the husband's chain of reflections. The larger poem presents his developing attitudes in three distinct parts: sonnets 1 through 26 show him reacting passively to her unfaithfulness; in sonnets 27 through 39 he tries to find a new partner; in sonnets 40 through 50 he moves from the "Lady" back to the wife, realizes that though physical love between them is irrevocably dead, she is worthy of his respect and affection, and finds the basis for a desired spiritual union destroyed by misunderstandings. The first part draws a number of domestic scenes that reveal the alienation between the couple: the unnatural silence and rigidity of the two partners on their marital bed and her suppression of sobs; her splendid appearance as she emerges from a session with the hairdresser and causes him to see "with eyes of other men" (sonnet 7); a visit from a newly engaged friend, whose overflowing happiness contrasts sharply with the dearth of their affections; a party, at which the couple dazzle not only their guests but even each other by the brilliance of their social performance:

> But here's the greater wonder; in that we
> Enamoured of an acting nought can tire,
> Each other, like true hypocrites, admire.
>
> (sonnet 17, 9–11)

Usually, the husband watches the wife, detects signs of duplicity— or thinks he does—and ponders on the attitude he should assume or on the implications of their personal tragedy for a general philosophy of life. He wanders brooding from one suggestive incident to another, from an event to an idea, or from seeing an experience in one light to seeing it in another. In part two he seeks distraction. In one sonnet (28) he feels the "promptings of Satanic power" like a Byronic hero flinging himself into the "sweet new world" of adultery; in the next, he asks himself: "Am I failing?" because adultery obviously does not cure him of his despair. Although the "Lady" is beautiful and has wit and common sense, she cannot help him re-create the glory love has had for him in the past. At one point it seems as if the old magic were still possible with the new partner: after the Lady has yielded to him, he walks through the woods, apostrophizing the moon as the "visage of still music in the sky" and feeling himself in harmony with the music of nature. But then he sees his wife and her lover, and harmony and magic flee, dispelled by overwhelming jealousy. No wonder that he exclaims, "What's my drift?" The multiplicity of attitudes evident in "Modern Love" attests a confusion of values and perceptions rarely expressed so compactly and effectively in Victorian fiction.

To underline this confusion Meredith uses a number of striking symbols. Certain groups of metaphors recur throughout the poem.[14] Most prominent are those connected with death, from the image of the marriage bed as a tomb in sonnet 1 to the midnight ocean of the last sonnet. These symbols not only signify the death of the couple's marriage but also foreshadow the wife's actual death by suicide. Poison is an anticipatory symbol as well as an image of the insidious nature of mutual distrust. The violence of the husband's emotions, particularly in his disillusionment, is conveyed by his frequent use of such terms as *murder, knife, wound,* and *blood.* For example, in a stunning juxtaposition of nature's fertility and the failure of their marriage, he accuses his wife of having slain their future:

> There wilt thou see
> An amber cradle near the sun's decline:
> Within it, featured even in death divine,
> Is lying a dead infant, slain by thee.
> (sonnet 11, 13–16)

In other places he associates the woman with witches and snakes, and his own unconquerable fascination with her, as well as his sexual frustration, is reflected in images of captivity and entrapment. But the flexibility of the metaphors allows for transfers: while the snake imagery at first applies to the woman and what her husband considers her devious behavior, he adopts it for himself in sonnet 26:

> A subtle serpent then has Love become.
> I had the eagle in my bosom erst:
> Henceforward with the serpent I am cursed

and the image of entrapment pertains to both partners in sonnet 50.

Not unnaturally, sexual passion appears in animal imagery. The husband sees himself as a "wild beast" with "teeth to rend" (sonnet 9). But animal metaphors can also represent the wholesomeness of nature. Moreover, by juxtaposing scenes of joyful animal activity with brooding reflections by the man (sonnets 10, 11, 12), Meredith indicates the sterility of the couple's present life. Sonnet 11, which describes a walk through the spring countryside, is structured on this contrast. Nature's beauty and fertility are the same as always; the woman's unfaithfulness, however, has changed them—apparently irrevocably—in his eyes. But sonnet 11 is not the last word on Nature; in fact, it is answered by sonnet 47, one of the undisputed masterpieces among Meredith's sonnets:

> We saw the swallows gathering in the sky,
> And in the osier-isle we heard them noise.
> We had not to look back on summer joys,
> Or forward to a summer of bright eye:
> But in the largeness of the evening earth
> Our spirits grew as we went side by side.
> The hour became her husband and my bride.
> Love that had robbed us so, thus blessed our dearth!
> The pilgrims of the year waxed very loud
> In multitudinous chatterings, as the flood
> Full brown came from the West, and like pale blood
> Expanded to the upper crimson cloud.
> Love that had robbed us of immortal things,
> This little moment mercifully gave,
> Where I have seen across the twilight wave
> The swan sail with her young beneath her wing.

In contrast to sonnet 11, this poem conveys a sense of rest and peace. It is an autumn scene; in her surface appearances, Nature *has* changed, but the speaker is aware of her underlying continuity. Consciousness of seasonal recurrence and sadness for the waste of their own lives come together in a beginning of spiritual growth. Characteristically, Meredith sees this growth primarily in a turning away from self-absorption to the simple observation of natural objects. Hence the sexual figures (husband, bride) are framed by autumnal ones. And while in sonnet 11 vernal metaphors clash with the symbol of the woman's "maternal" failure (the cradle in the sky), autumnal and maternal images join in sonnet 47—but not as artificial constructs by jaundiced human vision. Nature herself provides a symbol of eternity in change: the swan with her young.

The poem marks the husband's progress from denial to acceptance of change. For a moment he is able to immerse himself in a greater life, dominated by seasonal and generational rhythms and oblivious to human hopes, promises, or memories. What he is "mercifully" given is a moment of insight and quiet companionship. The poem seems to hold out the promise of a peaceful, companionable evening for the couple's lives.

That the moment of peace is fleeting, that the "I" of the insight seems to signal an exclusiveness of vision not boding well for sustained companionship, that the very next sonnet again mingles blame, bewilderment, self-doubt, and affection and again uses the ominous images of poison and entrapment—all this demonstrates Meredith's psychological sensitivity and his refusal to allow his characters an easy way out of their dilemma. Moreover, the fact that the final tragedy is brought about by "the pure daylight of honest speech" tellingly reaffirms the Meredithian skepticism about human discourse. "Modern Love" itself contradicts this skepticism; in contrast to many of Meredith's later poems, it is able—impressively so—to say what the poet desires.

Meredith's subject, "worth the serious interest of men," as Swinburne admiringly wrote to the *Spectator*,[15] as well as the subtlety and allusiveness of his method have continued to engage critical discussion. The poem has survived the reversals of taste and critical standards that led to the general neglect of Meredith's other poetry in this century. In its sensitivity to psychological shifts and undercurrents and in its awareness of linguistic instabilities, it speaks to twentieth-century readers—more than it did to his contemporaries. Indeed, the work has taken its place with the important long poems of the nineteenth century and the great sonnet cycles of the English language.

Chapter Three

Early Fiction: New Novels for an "Acute and Honourable Minority"

After Meredith's unsuccessful debut as a poet in 1851, he turned to prose fiction in order to support his family and make a name for himself. In the twelve years between *The Shaving of Shagpat* (1855) and *Vittoria* (1867) he wrote five novels and two prose narratives of shorter length. Although he showed some indebtedness to Sterne, Fielding, Peacock, Carlyle, and the German Jean Paul Richter—particularly in his parodying of romance and in his frequent insertion of authorial comment—Meredith sought from the beginning to establish a voice and method of his own. He intended to make the novel as effective a medium for serious thought as poetry and to incorporate in prose fiction the ideas he stressed in his verse: the beauty and sanity of nature; man's need to maintain in himself a healthy balance of blood, brain, and spirit; and the advancement of civilization through an individual's devoted service to the common good. To transmit these ideas to his audience he combined in his fiction the qualities of the poet, the philosopher, the historian, and the writer of comedy.

In an important passage in *The Ordeal of Richard Feverel,* his earliest novel, Meredith points out what he sees as the most useful quality of a novel: its ability to probe beneath the surface of events and demonstrate underlying causes and connections, particularly among the motivations from which man's vital decisions spring:

At present, I am aware, an audience impatient for Blood and Glory scorns the stress I am putting on incidents so minute, a picture so little imposing. One will come to whom it will be given to see the elementary machinery at work, who, as it were, from some slight hint of the straws, will feel the winds of March when they do not blow. To them nothing will be trivial, seeing that they will have in their eyes the invisible conflict going on around us, whose features a nod, a smile, a laugh of ours perpetually changes. And

47

they will perceive, moreover, that in real life all hangs together: the train is laid in the lifting of an eyebrow, that bursts upon the field of thousands. They will see the links of things as they pass, and wonder not, as foolish people now do, that this great matter came out of that small one.[1]

The passage announces a radical divergence from traditional rules in fiction. Meredith rejects the conventional emphasis on sensational or highly dramatic scenes. For him, plot is the vehicle for the revelations of a character's deepest emotions; these revelations take precedence over external events. Thus his novels lack the conventional straight-forward narrative movement. Events are often mentioned and explained retrospectively, in an aside likely to escape the reader's attention.

Apart from stressing the analytical quality of his fiction, the passage is significant for some other points. It shows Meredith's confidence in the evolution of a more perceptive readership—a major part of his general evolutionary optimism. It is characterized by a rather belligerent tone: the writer sets himself deliberately against his present audience, pronouncing it deficient in awareness. At other places—for example, in *Evan Harrington*—Meredith ironically emphasizes the present generation's "purity"; or, in response to critics who charged him with elitism, he denounces the lowering of literary standards to the present levels of farce or sensationalism. His attitude toward his readers—shifting between aggressiveness and self-defensiveness—is an essential component of his writings.[2]

Second, the above passage illustrates Meredith's penchant for imagery. His far-ranging and often proliferating metaphors are evident in his prose as well as in his poetry, although he may satirize pretentiously picturesque language in his characters. As in his verse, Meredith's imagery is often aesthetically jarring and intellectually challenging. More frequently it imitates the free-flowing, semiconscious associations constantly occurring in a person's mind. In effect, his imagery tends to blur the borders between the inner life of his protagonists and the outer life of the story—or the mind of the narrator. In Meredith's later work the fusion between inner and outer life becomes progressively more marked.

In another respect Meredith keeps the line between protagonist and narrator firmly in place. The very fact that a passage like the one cited occurs in the middle of a chapter entitled "In Which the Hero Takes a Step"—an important departure for the protagonist—suggests that the writer is not intent on maintaining an unbroken narrative line. He sets up his play of "puppets"—the image, a direct borrowing from Thackeray, recurs often in his novels—only to disrupt it by overt authorial comment.[3] On the one hand, he draws his audience into the very center of his plots; on the other, he considers his characters scientific objects—"the elementary machinery at work." While asserting the truthfulness of their conception, he stresses their fictionality and sets them into a long literary tradition, emphasized frequently through the phrasing of his chapter titles. By making his characters both plausibly human and recognizably literary, he calls in question the literary conventions and the assumptions on which they are based.

The intervention of the narrator is, of course, not a new phenomenon. Fielding, whom Meredith admired, had used it frequently and effectively; in the nineteenth century, it appeared rather indiscriminately. Meredith's contribution to this tradition is a measure of ambiguity and tension. Since he has not, like Fielding, the approval of a commonsensical audience, he often resorts to overstatement masking a defensive attitude, which he then punctures with self-irony. And although he urges a "scientific" study of his heroes, he is as suspicious of a purely intellectual approach to his material as of an unthinkingly emotional one. These contradictory elements enter into the authorial intrusions, sometimes in the form of regular debates. Or the actions and reactions of his "puppets" themselves call in question the value of his comments. *The Ordeal of Richard Feverel,* for example, offers several instances of the unreliability of "scientific" attitudes, and in *Sandra Belloni* the Philosopher is put in his place by the inanity of the supremely philosophical couple Cornelia Pole and Purcell Barrett.

Meredith's ironic method suggests in itself a key theme of his fiction, the contrast between theory and reality. In the framework of his novels this contrast becomes a conflict—the "invisible conflict" of the passage quoted—between retarding and progressive human impulses. Put in simple terms, man's urge to grow into a higher spiritual life is pitted against the forces chaining him to his lower nature—moral shortsightedness, laziness, and vanity. It is also a conflict between Nature, which demands man's constant adjustment and development, and society, which tends to inhibit growth because it shelters the individual from self-discovery. In Meredith's novels socially fashionable attitudes, such as sentimentalism and cynicism, collide with experiences calling for a truthful and committed response.

"Society" for Meredith means the gentry, the class with money and leisure to pursue a life favorable to the "fine Shades" and "nice Feelings" he ridicules in *Sandra Belloni*. In the second half of the nineteenth century, economic prosperity and political weight shrank the distance between the upper and the middle class. In many ways the middle class with aspirations toward gentility behaved more "aristocratically" than did the aristocracy itself, as Meredith points out with devastating comedy in *Evan Harrington* and *Sandra Belloni*. To assume the life-style of the gentry and enjoy the refinements of prosperity (of which luxuriousness of feeling is a major part) without a corresponding sense of social obligation—this behavior furnishes material for Meredith's comic scrutiny.

Specifically, he focuses on two groups within society: the young man of privileged background and the intelligent young woman. The novels' protagonists face the task of discovering how they can participate in the world's forward movement. Usually, Nature has equipped them well enough: they are healthy, bright, idealistic. But what society offers them to exercise their talents is not much more than the models of the "dashing" gentleman and the "clever" hostess—well-bred, frivolous dilettantes. They are vaguely dissatisfied with these models. They see themselves as destined for great deeds but restrained by circumstances; they regularly invoke "fate." And here Meredith presents a fundamental paradox: their own consciousness of superiority, their own eagerness to advance the world and champion a brilliant cause, makes them forget that they are part of the world and, at least partly, implicated in its deficiencies. Reality must not encroach upon their aspirations. The narrator observes of Wilfrid Pole: "He could pledge himself to eternity, but shrank from being bound to eleven o'clock on the morrow morning" (*Sandra Belloni*, 1:202). This self-contradictory attitude reveals itself first to the reader and eventually to the protagonists themselves when they face ordeals involving their total personality.

Love is the most trying of the ordeals Meredith imposes on them to test the extent and strength of their idealism. Such factors as social status and finances play into their choices; Meredith reveals the multiplicity of their motives as well as the strategies they employ to hide this multiplicity from themselves. In the course of their ordeals the protagonists find that fate cannot serve as an excuse for the neglect of real responsibilities or that their heroism masks a weakness that makes them just as human as their neighbors. Some of them come to grips with their humanity; others, too much sheltered by social conventions, continue to evade self-knowledge, with disastrous consequences for themselves and others. Since they are by nature neither worthless nor unattractive, but, rather, spirited and high-minded, Meredith regards their failure as potentially tragic. His compassion, however, is tempered by irony, most concisely expressed in the oxymoronic chapter title "The Tragedy of Sentiment" for Sir Purcell's suicide (*Sandra Belloni*, 2:258). The sentimental hero who "plays" at life is not really worthy of the tragic mask. In authorial comments as well as in his use of mock heroic language Meredith points out how ludicrous a character becomes when he consciously sets himself apart from his fellowmen. Idealism without a firm basis in self-knowledge, Meredith asserts, may be pitiful, but it is also absurd.

Behind this ironic view lies Meredith's concept of the writer's double role as moralist and psychologist. As an evolutionist, he believed that Nature had equipped man with the elasticity of body and mind to live happily and usefully. Thus if man failed to take advantage of his powers, if he let his senses overrule his brain, he was to be held morally accountable: circumstances might mitigate his guilt but not excuse it. As a psychologist, Meredith was interested in the way virtues pervert themselves by excess and distortion. None of his characters harbors gross moral vices; they mean well, but feeding on the complacency of a prosperous society, their virtues get out of shape and require a serious spiritual jolt for a healthy trimming. Meredith suggests that these ordeals are natural stages of growth undergone, more or less drastically, by every person, usually in youth but sometimes later. What he is not prepared to explain is why some people persist in self-deception. More precisely, he does not admit the "fate" of heredity and environment as more than a partial excuse. He is generous with causes for psychological aberrations and precise in the notation of their growth, but he does not allow the reader to forget the preeminence of the moral will.

In part, Meredith's early novels are self-exorcisms. During his twenties and thirties he was undergoing ordeals of his own. The questions he addresses—how to find, in the given framework of society, a healthy approach to sexual love and a place to realize one's talents adequately and honorably—were particularly urgent to him. His fiction at this time plays out variations of possible answers. Self-dramatization is, so Meredith frequently demonstrates, a strategy of the sentimental hero. Self-dramatization refracted through irony removes the stigma of sentimentalism and allows Meredith to "place" his perplexities.

Beyond these issues the early novels introduce an ongoing exploration of the writer's tools, goals, and liabilities. Meredith the writer becomes a participant in his plots. He exploits the tension between disinterested intellectual inquiry, the pursuit of moral progress, and the search for aesthetic perfection. Pointing out the limitations of a purely aesthetic or purely didactic perspective, he warns his readers as well as himself that a sentimental or prejudiced disregard of these limitations renders one vulnerable to the corrective laughter of common sense. This insistence on an ironic approach to his material, his craft, his audience, and himself makes Meredith's novels distinctive among mid-Victorian literature.

The Shaving of Shagpat

Meredith's debut as a prose writer was unusual. Unlike most young authors, who turn to autobiographical material for their first book, he offered a narrative remote in form and content from his life, his culture, and the conventions of realistic fiction. When he published *The Shaving of Shagpat* in 1855, critics were charmed but puzzled what to make of it.

As its subtitle, *An Arabian Entertainment,* indicates, the story takes place in the Middle East. Like a traditional epic it starts in medias res, briefly introducing the name and genealogy of its hero and then plunging right into the action; much later, background material is added. The hero, Shibli Bagarag, is a barber whose task it is to shave off a particular hair from the head of Shagpat, a clothier. The hair, called "the Identical," has magical properties, and the task amounts to an enormous ordeal, testing Shibli's persistence, loyalty, and humility. In the course of his trial Shibli undergoes all kinds of temptations, especially to his vanity, and shows himself yielding rather easily. Punishment follows swiftly and unmistakably in the form of "thwackings" (physical beatings) or enchantments. But Shibli has a protectress in Noorna, a benign sorceress, whom he has promised to marry even in the disguise of an old crone. In the end he successfully shaves the "Identical" and lives happily ever after with Noorna, now a beautiful princess.

Pages of summary cannot recount in detail all of Shibli's adventures. Even after a few readings it is hard to remember when a particular person appears in what form or function. One of the salient features of the book is that Shibli wanders through a fairy-tale setting that generates event after event. Added to the main plot are three subplots in the form of interpolated stories. Just what the meaning of the main plot is supposed to be, however, remains a matter of critical debate.

Many Victorians and later readers have taken the subtitle at its word and enjoyed the story as an Arabian "entertainment"—a dazzling display of inventiveness and stylistic dexterity. The story is not only a fairy tale but also a mock epic, complete with Homeric, Biblical, and medieval echoes. For example, the dignity of the introductory genealogy of the hero is undercut by Shibli's and Shagpat's mundane occupations:

It was ordained that Shibli Bagarag, nephew to the renowned Baba Mustapha, chief barber to the court of Persia, should shave Shagpat, the son of Shimpoor, the son of Shoolpi, the son of Shullum; and they had been clothiers for generations, even to the time of Shagpat, the illustrious.[4]

Throughout the book Shibli's most trivial concerns are presented in an elevated style, frequently underscored by authorial comment in verse, which adds the weight of "antiquity." Extended Homeric similes interrupt the narrative, and true to epic tradition, weapons are described in detail, but the Sword of Aklis, acquired by Shibli in the face of extraordinary dangers, functions most heroically as a barber's knife in shaving his enemy's hair!

Since Oriental and pseudomedieval tales were very popular in Victorian fiction, Meredith's mock epic may be seen as a vigorous spoof of this fad. From the beginning, however, readers attempted to find more in it than that. As Meredith's humorous disclaimer in the foreword to the second edition makes clear, it seemed to many to be an allegory; at least one full-scale contemporary study worked out a consistent allegorical pattern.[5] Meredith himself humorously stated that allegories were "mortal," that is, short-lived, and in their requirement of absolute clarity "as little attractive as Mrs. Malaprop's reptile."[6] But such names as "the Identical" for Shagpat's magic hair, Noorna's mysterious self-definition as "that I shall be," and the title "Mistress of Illusions" for an evil sorceress suggest that the tale has at least symbolic resonance. Obviously, it shows the testing and maturing of a young man through many ordeals until he has learned to rid himself of presumptuousness and is able to detect truth behind the illusions of the senses. Meredith also seems to suggest that truth is not an absolute, and if treated as such—as the "Identical" is unquestioningly venerated by the people—it induces mental sloth and stupidity. Although self-knowledge leads to liberation (Shibli frees himself from the imprisonment of his vanity when he beholds himself in a mirror as crowned with asses' ears), too much knowledge can be deadly: flashing his sword against a veiled figure, Shibli suddenly finds himself face to face with the terrifying truth of the "Mistress of the Illusions." He is saved from insanity only through his beloved Noorna's devoted nursing in an underground cave flowing with water—obviously a symbol of death and rebirth through love. Like the water cave, many details in *Shagpat* recall literary archetypes and myths, placing Shibli's exploits in a common tradition of fictional self-exploration. In this respect, the ambiguously attractive women of the tale are particularly significant, suggesting that Meredith— perhaps from his unhappy marriage—had ambivalent feelings about beautiful enchantresses.[7]

Shagpat can be read as fictional self-exploration in several respects. In the few years of his marriage Meredith may well have pondered the mystery of Mary Nicolls's "bewitching" attraction. He was also clarifying his professional goals. He shared the romantics' conviction that the poet was the spiritual leader of his time, but that to achieve that distinction he must first purge himself of pride. As a young poet, Meredith was still unsure of his worth, and the lukewarm reception of his *Poems* in 1851 had not reassured him. Shibli Bagarag, an initially unpromising hero, endures a number of setbacks that reduce his vanity and strengthen his common sense. He gains a beautiful wife, but, more prominently in the narrative, he dis-enchants a great number of bewitched people and ultimately releases an entire city from the spell of mindless adoration. Shibli the barber can be seen as the poet who modestly but radically brings about a spiritual revolution of society. Thus, *The Shaving of Shagpat* dramatizes both the trials and the rewards Meredith saw in his chosen path.

In its main ideas, its handling of style and structure, and its pervasive irony, *Shagpat* has close affinities with Carlyle's *Sartor Resartus* (1833), although it lacks the earlier book's depth of vision and overt social criticism. Like Carlyle's work, *Shagpat* resists simple categorizing. The myth of self-discovery, so central to the romantic imagination, appears here in the form of parody. Meredith heaps disdain on the "single-thoughted"; Noorna's particular talent is to be "double-thoughted," to recognize contradictory aspects beneath the smooth surface of illusions. Irony and paradox govern the narrative from the tongue-in-cheek preface to the concluding summary of Shibli's reign as barber-king and protector of women. It is not self-destructive irony since it upholds, inside the story and in the narrative texture, the restorative power of laughter. But Meredith warns his audience as well as himself that an uncritical devotion to fictional self-exploration, without comic detachment, can come dangerously close to the folly Shibli is shown by the mirror in the palace of illusions.[8]

The Ordeal of Richard Feverel: A History of a Father and Son

Meredith's first full-length novel, *The Ordeal of Richard Feverel*, shows the impact of the intellectual ferment characterizing the 1850s. It appeared in 1859, the year that also saw the publication of Darwin's *Origin of Species* and George Eliot's *Adam Bede*. Eliot's concern with involving the reader in serious topical issues and complex analysis is shared by the author of *Richard Feverel*. The topics of heredity, environmental influence, and eugenics, central to evolutionary discussion, resonate through Meredith's novel. A related issue—the value of educational systems and their effect on parents and children—which had been explored by Herbert Spencer in the *British Quarterly Review* in 1858, provides the focus from which Meredith approaches the history of the Feverels.

As its subtitle indicates, *Richard Feverel* centers on two characters, Richard and his father, Sir Austin Feverel. The first third of the novel focuses more on Sir Austin than on Richard; it is predominantly comic in outlook and originally contained broadly farcical material Meredith eliminated in the 1878 edition.[9] Richard's "ordeal," as much for his father as himself, begins when he is eighteen and falls in love; from then on the novel takes a tragic turn, although its unforgiving outcome has seemed excessively severe to many readers.

Sir Austin, deserted by his wife, brings up his only son according to a particular system of scientific principles. Since he believes that women have had disastrous effects on the Feverel men—a belief rooted in his own experience but elevated to a pseudoscientific "dogma"—he attempts to keep Richard away from sexual temptation by educating him at home and rigorously banning from his estate all behavior suggesting romantic emotions. Richard grows up knowing virtually nothing about women, but having exalted notions about his role in society and the duties connected with it. At eighteen—seven years earlier than his father's system prescribes—he meets and falls in love with the niece of a neighboring farmer, Lucy. The two young people marry secretly in London. Sir Austin refuses to acknowledge Lucy as a daughter-in-law. When Richard attempts a reconciliation, he holds the young man off and keeps him separated from his wife for months. During this time he arranges for Richard to become involved with questionable company in order that he might get to know "the world." Richard conceives himself a rescuer of fallen women, but it is he who falls, seduced by Bella Mount, who plays on his vanity.

Clare Forney, his devoted cousin, whom he has upbraided for submitting to a loveless marriage, commits suicide because she feels unworthy of Richard's further respect. Faced with this tragedy, Richard realizes his guilt toward both Lucy and Claire, and ashamed to face his wife, he goes to the Continent with vague ideas of redeeming himself through some heroic action. While he tarries in the Rhineland, his cousin Austin Wentworth brings him news that Lucy has borne him a son and is now accepted by his father. The existence of his child urges him home. But an outdated letter by Bella Mount, informing him that her estranged husband had schemed to seduce Lucy, incites him to challenge that nobleman to a duel. He has barely time to see his child and be assured of Lucy's forgiveness before he is seriously wounded in the duel. Lucy, kept from him on the insistence of Sir Austin, whose "system" now demands her single-minded attention to her baby, breaks down by this renewed separation and dies of brain fever.

This synopsis, which makes the novel appear rather melodramatic, may suggest that Meredith's main concern is to indict a particular educational system—such as Rousseau's, with which Sir Austin's has some similarity.[10] But even within the book Meredith states explicitly that the system has been successful up to a point: it has led Richard to choose the right mate for himself. In a letter to Samuel Lucas, Meredith explains where the real cause of the Feverel tragedy lies: "The moral is that no System of the sort succeeds with human nature, unless the originator has conceived it purely independent of personal passion. That was Sir Austin's way of wreaking his revenge" (*Letters*, 1:40).

What interests Meredith here is the way characters and ideas—particularly fashionable ideas—interact. He is less interested in the ideas themselves than in their impact on sensitive, intelligent characters whose very intelligence and sensitivity are likely to block their spontaneous reactions. In *Richard Feverel* both father and son are such characters, one faced with the problem of how to raise a child to perfection, and the other, how to translate this perfection into an active life. The comedy and the tragedy of the novel come from the unrealistic concept of perfection both men nourish. Since the perfectibility of the human species according to scientific systems was much debated among Victorian intellectuals, Sir Austin shows himself a man of his period; as for Richard and his search for knightly feats, the narrator exclaims, "Alas for the hero in our time!"

In creating Sir Austin and Richard, Meredith was using elements from his own life, but managed to handle them with considerable objectivity. Sir Austin's marital history resembles his own, and in the occasional gibes against Lady Feverel's lover as well as the shadowiness of Lady Feverel herself, one detects traces of Meredith's resentment. But in this novel the marital history appears in the more general context of human follies and delusions, and as the portrayal of Sir Austin shows, Meredith—if he identified himself with the baronet—did not spare himself. Though he presents the facts that seem to exonerate Sir Austin from all blame in the marital disaster, he also insinuates, by a skillful modulation of voice, that the roots of it, and of the ensuing tragedy, are in Sir Austin himself.

As Gillian Beer has shown, this modulating occurs even in the earliest account of the past events.[11] Sir Austin has, like Meredith, lost his wife to a minor artist and has not forgiven her. Deceptively terse background information is given by the narrator: "He had a wife, and he had a friend. His marriage was for love; his wife was a beauty; his friend was a sort of poet. His wife had his whole heart, and his friend all his confidence" (4). A little later the tone changes, suddenly echoing Shakespeare and Keats and revealing strong emotion:

Such was the outline of the story. But the baronet could fill it up. He had opened his soul to these two. He had been noble Love to the one, and to the other perfect Friendship. He had bid them be brother and sister whom he loved, and live a Golden Age with him at Raynham. In fact, he had been prodigal of the excellences of his nature, which it is not good to be, and, like Timon, he became bankrupt, and fell upon bitterness. (5)

The sequence of sentences beginning with "He" is rather insistent, implying that the baronet's "filling up" the story is clearly one-sided. And the capitalization of *Love, Friendship,* and *Golden Age* suggests that Sir Austin himself is in the habit of using these terms; the entire passage comes across as a self-defensive internal monologue recited by the baronet whenever he meditates on the history of his marriage. As such, it reveals not only Sir Austin's erudition but also his egocentricity. The rest of the novel corroborates this impression.

One important aspect, which he shares, not incidentally, with Meredith, is his propensity to aphorism. Excerpts of his collection of epigrams—the "Pilgrim's Scrip"—are interspersed throughout the novel, frequently by the narrator as a clever commentary. Aphorisms usually distill experience into succinct, authoritative insights. In *Richard Feverel* their function is more complex. Often they underscore the irony informing Sir Austin's history: the wise man cannot apply his wisdom to himself. The aphorisms are sometimes explicitly endorsed by the narrator, and Gillian Beer has shown that some have come directly from Meredith's notebooks.[12] Others show Sir Austin blatantly wrongheaded, particularly in his attitude toward women. He has gathered the experience of his marriage into a collection of misogynistic statements to support the more questionable tenets of his educational system.

The whole issue of Sir Austin's authorship stands for a larger one: his monumental arrogance. The baronet believes that he can reduce life to a "system," manage "Fortune and the Fates," and create a New Man in a New Paradise. Meredith's juxtaposition of aphorisms and the events of the story devastatingly puts Sir Austin in his place for the reader.

The turning point of Sir Austin's psychological history occurs in a brilliantly executed scene following his discovery that Richard has married Lucy. Since it is the first time that his son has gone against his will, he is devastated: apparently his system has failed, and the Feverel "ordeal" has not been exorcised despite all his care. His first, supremely self-incriminating reaction is: "It is useless to base any System on a human being" (331). Meredith's remark to Lucas—that such systems succeed only when free from any individual's "personal passion"—comes immediately to mind; the contrast between Sir Austin's sweeping conclusion and Meredith's carefully qualified observation lights up Sir Austin's ultimate flaw:

A Manichaean tendency, from which the sententious eulogist of Nature had been struggling for years (and which was partly at the bottom of the System), now began to cloud and usurp dominion of his mind. As he sat alone in the forlorn dead-hush of his library, he saw the Devil. (333)

The last image marks the transition from a poignant personal disappointment ("Richard was no longer the Richard of his creation") to a fundamental conflict between good and evil in his soul. Meredith puts his protagonist at the center of a transcendental system based not on "Fortune and the Fates," as Sir Austin would have it, but on his psychological "tendencies." In his dialogue with the malignant spirit the baronet reveals his contempt for humanity and for a science that does not gratify his self-image. In this scene Sir Austin faces his real ordeal, and because he cannot relinquish his pride, he fails it. Comic in his arrogance, pathetic in his effort to preserve a stiff upper lip, he comes across to the reader as a complex yet believable figure.

Meredith's autobiographical interest in the younger Feverel derives from his own unsettled career and uncertain prospects. Because his handling of Sir Austin is so convincing, one tends to forget that Meredith himself, when he wrote the novel, was only thirty and by no means an established writer. He had also just experienced the breakup of his marriage. Like Richard, he had been a solitary, indulged but motherless child; he was now raising another motherless child, his son by Mary Nicolls. One can surmise also that in retrospect he saw his own impetuous wooing of Mary when barely out of his teens as a rather foolish undertaking. In short, he was able to understand the young protagonist's sense of an exceptional destiny and his frantic effort to find an object for his heroism in a world little interested in the exceptional or heroic.

Although Richard shows a proud disposition and harbors romantic fantasies in his "Blossoming Age," Meredith gives few hints that he will end by destroying his own and several other lives. On the whole, Richard's youth is pleasant, and many of Sir Austin's pedagogical ideas—for instance, his emphasis on sports—have Meredith's obvious approval. But ironically, the System is most successful at the one stage Sir Austin would like to postpone: Richard's own unspoilt nature finds a suitable object for his emerging sexual instincts when he meets Lucy.

The beauty and wholesomeness of this encounter are expressed through some remarkable lyrical passages in chapters 15 and 19. But the poetry of these scenes is qualified by ominous mock-heroic imagery. The two are Adam and Eve before the Fall. They are also Ferdinand and Miranda, of Shakespeare's *Tempest,* discovering in each other a brave new world—the references here are explicit, along with the foreboding remark that Sir Austin is not Prospero. Finally, they are the knight of romance and his lady, whom he protects against evil dragons, such as his father's voyeuristic servant. This role is most congenial to Richard, and he maintains it even when fate, in the form of his father, has separated him from his love and supplied such dubious substitutes as the fallen women—his own mother and Bella Mount.

In the separation of Richard and Lucy many critics have seen a structural and psychological weakness of the novel. Although one understands Richard's desire to reestablish a close relationship with his father, it seems implausible that he should be willing to endure a months-long absence from her. During this time Lucy drops almost entirely out of view. Thematically, however, this absence makes sense: Meredith sees Richard as a man of two unreconciled natures—one wholesome, one spoilt and arrogant—and the rest of the novel is largely a record of Richard's internal conflict, unresolved till the very end. In this shift from the "New Comedy" of the first part of the novel to Richard's ordeal in the second, the scene of his seduction by Bella Mount is crucial, not just because it marks his "fall," but because it ironically comments on the romance of the "Ferdinand and Miranda" scene. With its highly artificial disguises, sexual ambiguities, and literary allusions, it functions as a counterpart to Lucy and Richard's first meeting; more directly than the narrator's mock-heroic language in the earlier scene it highlights the spurious character of Richard's "heroism."

It is important to note that Meredith does not make Richard's fall an unpardonable sin, although Richard himself does. In the chapter "Nature Speaks" the young man gets another chance. He is purged of his pretensions (a thunderstorm metaphorically washes them away) and reconnected to Lucy through news of his child's birth. At first he responds to the thunderstorm with Byronic enthusiasm for the grand spectacle, but gradually Nature's other side, that of a maternal tenderness, reaches him: a small rabbit he has picked up and carries in his pocket affectionately begins to lick his hand. He responds with sudden and quite overwhelming feelings of release and love. With the symbol of a rustic roadside Madonna, Meredith indicates Richard's apparent rebirth and his place in the eternal natural experience of parenthood.

Because the catharsis in "Nature Speaks" is powerfully and convincingly conveyed, it comes as a shock to the reader that the novel does not end with the scene of reconciliation between Richard and Lucy. We expect a happy end, not only because of the psychological impact of the preceding event, but also because literary convention has taught us that moral conversions are total, permanent, and rewarded with domestic bliss. Meredith, however, insists on thwarting our expectations for the sake of psychological realism: a single insight, however powerful, does not usually negate almost twenty years of a rigorously applied educational system. Richard comes home, still very much divided in nature and unchanged in his most disturbing quality, his pride. Unable to face, even now, the fact that human nature is neither angelic nor devilish, and therefore also unable to forgive himself, he turns his self-contempt into a rage against Lord Mountfalcon, Lucy's would-be seducer. His debate over whether or not to pursue the lord recalls his father's dialogue with the devil; again fate, rather than personal failure, is made the villain of the story. Some readers have objected to the fact that it is Lucy rather than Richard who dies.[13] Here again Meredith opts for psychological realism rather than literary convention. One of the main points the novel makes is that sentimentalists indulge their emotions without regard for the results of their behavior. Richard is the victim of Sir Austin's pride; Lucy that of Richard's. And as if to reconfirm Sir Austin's part in the whole tragedy, Meredith makes him technically responsible for Lucy's death; characteristically, he has adopted a "system" to raise his grandson—a system that denies, as his former system did, the reality of human feelings and thus frustrates Lucy's natural desire to be with her husband.

Meredith's method of first building up and then thwarting the reader's expectations of conventional plots and outcomes informs all his novels. But it is particularly insistent in *Richard Feverel,* partly because Meredith, as a new author, was self-consciously asserting himself against the more established novelists, especially Dickens. More important, this method underlines the message of the novel itself. It warns the reader against applying a "system" of literary conventions, based on the sentimentalism of unthinking and rigid adherence to tradition. Richard, Meredith makes clear, is not a puppet—not his father's, or fate's, or the novel's (despite the Thackerayan metaphor in chapter 25). In fact, Meredith's ironic insistence on the fictionality of his "hero" aims at the complacency of the reader who looks to the novel for easily understandable characters, easily predictable outcomes, and easily deducible moral messages.

Like most of Meredith's novels, *Richard Feverel* contains a great number of subordinate characters. Most important is Adrian Harley, Richard's cousin and tutor, called the "Wise Youth" by the baronet. In Adrian, Meredith presents the moral extreme of complete selfishness coupled with a cynical intelligence. He is an "epicurean of our modern notions," whose heart resides in his stomach. Because of his wit, Adrian is the darling of society, but beneath his polished exterior lurks a Mephistophelian tendency toward mischief making that contributes decisively toward the Feverel tragedy. Adrian looks on life as an endless comedy. While the narrator often imitates his tone of worldly amusement, the novel as a whole contradicts and rejects his contemptuous and ultimately irresponsible point of view.[14]

At the opposite end of the moral spectrum is Austin Wentworth, the first of a line of Meredithian socially responsible, commonsensical heroes. Whenever he appears, he brings out the best in Richard. Unobtrusively, he sets things right, as far as he can. In contrast to Adrian, he is not socially popular, except with a few women who recognize his innate goodness.

Among the women in the novel three are typical of Meredith's female figures. Lucy is his unspoilt child of nature, physically and emotionally healthy, with native good breeding. She is also inexperienced and thus unable to assert herself against Richard's follies and the schemes of the more sophisticated characters. No other woman in Meredith's fiction is such a defenseless victim of male sentimentality; his later female characters either are somewhat implicated in their downfall or—by far the majority—combine natural innocence with the resilience to throw off destructive relationships.

Mrs. Berry, Richard's former nurse, is the representative of "plain folk." But Meredith had little experience of lower-class people, and here, as in many other novels, he creates a caricature instead of a believable character. Like the Nurse in *Romeo and Juliet,* she supports young love and contributes a measure of earthiness to the story. But she is sickeningly sentimental (in the modern sense) and garrulous.

Lady Blandish, on the other hand, is a successful characterization of another Meredithian type: the basically sensible older woman of society. She starts out as one of Sir Austin's uncritical admirers. Meredith's most famous epigram, "Sentimentalists are they who seek to enjoy Reality without incurring the Immense Debtorship for a thing done" (213), is directed at her, because she flirts with the baronet without honestly examining her feelings. But from the start she shows consideration for others. She respects Austin Wentworth. When Sir Austin refuses to forgive his son, she begins to understand and pity him for the weakness underlying his pride. At the end it is she who describes Lucy's death. Writing to Austin Wentworth, she makes it clear that she has lost all admiration for the "scientific humanist" and finds it hard to see him charitably. To give her the last word in the novel shows Meredith's excellent judgment; her exasperation with Sir Austin, mingled with grief at the wreckage father and son have wrought, conveys the novel's humane outlook better than the objective narrator's analysis could.

The Ordeal of Richard Feverel did not find much favor, popular or critical. Reviewers were concerned either with the system, which they took to be the main topic of the novel, or with the issue of purity, since Meredith had described Richard's seduction in some detail. The second issue had immediate practical consequences for Meredith, since Mudie's Circulating Library withdrew the book from its list after a few readers had complained about its immorality. Critics in the *Times* and the *Saturday Review* conceded that the seduction chapter had nothing prurient about it, but few readers were willing to expose their families to knowledge of the existence of sexual degradation. The *Saturday Review's* insistence that this was a "man's book" only underscored, in a more subtle form, the view that led Mudie to reject it.[15]

The fact that many critics apparently thought the system's failure was Meredith's main argument justifies his suspicions of his audience. It suggested that people did not read carefully and were impervious to irony more subtle than Dickensian humor or overt social satire. The reviewers failed to understand Meredith's manipulations of language and fictional conventions; they found *Richard Feverel* unsatisfactory both as a tract on education and as a realistic novel.

Evan Harrington

Stung by the failure of *Richard Feverel* and constrained by the policies of serial publication, Meredith made *Evan Harrington* (1860; serialized February–October in *Once a Week*) a fairly conventional novel. He addressed a topic of particular interest to the middle-class reading public: the effect of class distinctions on a character's moral development. Debates about the qualities of a "gentleman" and the possibility of crossing from the tradesman's into the upper middle class and vice versa had found their way into popular fiction, as Dickens's *Oliver Twist* and Dinah Mulock Craik's *John Halifax, Gentleman* show. These questions are not Meredith's primary issues; he is concerned with the effect of a preoccupation with class distinctions upon an immature mind. While *Evan Harrington* undeniably reflects his conviction that class lines should not be rigidly exclusive, it acknowledges the reality of social distinctions and comically exposes the ambitions, self-deceptions, and sentimental self-denials of those preoccupied with the value society puts upon them. In his protagonist he dramatizes the paradox that class distinctions can be transcended only when their reality is freely acknowledged; in the main female character he illustrates the obverse paradox that an insistence on social superiority in itself condemns the snob to inferiority.

Evan Harrington, a tailor's son brought up with expectations of a higher social position, returns from a vacation abroad in the company of a diplomat and his niece, Rose Jocelyn, whom the countess of Saldar, Evan's sister, would like to secure for Evan. The countess, as well as Evan's two other sisters, who have also married well, suppress their family background; the Jocelyns know nothing of Evan's roots in tailordom. At his arrival in London, Evan learns about his father's death. Facing the task of repaying his father's extensive debts, he grimly accedes to his mother's wish to take up the family business. The countess, however, secures his company on a visit to Rose's parents. The genteel life at Beckley Court and the attraction of Rose for a time weaken his resolve to fulfill his family obligations, and his sister's scheming—she intercepts, for example, a letter in which he reveals his background to Rose—puts him into an ambiguous position.

Rose learns about Evan's social status from other sources, and although he quickly clears himself of the suspicion of having courted her under false pretenses, it costs her some effort to overcome her own snobbery and accept him. Her parents, however, disapprove, and his mother appears at Beckley Court to recall him back to his duty. In addition, the countess, by forging a letter, destroys all chances for the lovers when Evan, to protect the family name, assumes responsibility for this duplicity. The Harringtons leave Beckley in disgrace; only Juliana Bonner, the sickly heiress of the estate, who is hopelessly in love with Evan, maintains his innocence. The countess manages to keep up this connection and scheme further for her brother. When Juliana dies, Evan inherits the entire estate. He renounces the inheritance, earning the Jocelyns' gratitude and respect, regaining Rose's love, and clearing himself from any shadow of duplicity. He is now free to marry Rose, and a kindly though eccentric family friend even supplies him with enough money for the gentlemanly profession of attaché to Naples.

Evan Harrington draws more overtly on autobiographic material than *Richard Feverel;* Meredith's brilliant grandfather and socially ambitious aunts appear thinly disguised, and the Jocelyns are modeled on the Duff Gordons, aristocratic neighbors of Meredith, who treated the writer on equal social terms. Meredith's father saw himself in Evan and was deeply wounded, but it is more likely that Meredith intended Evan as a comic picture of his own social insecurity. To distance himself from the material, he set the novel about thirty years into the past and adopted a consistent perspective as a benign, worldly narrator, amused at the follies of the young "snip." "Our comedies are frequently youth's tragedies"[16] sums up the narrator's attitude. The plot seems to be governed by the question of whether society will find him out or whether he can escape ignominious exposure; for his sister this *is,* in fact, the only concern, but the protagonist is taught that the question of actual social position is less important than that of personal integrity.

The novel's subtitle, "He Would Be a Gentleman," sums up Evan's problem. He certainly would be a gentleman, both by desire and ability, if only he had not been born a tailor. His natural talents and upbringing qualify him for a higher position, as he is well aware. He shows the same romantic idealism as Richard Feverel, yearning for the Middle Ages when men could win their knighthood through heroic exploits. But Evan has inherited not only the "Presence" of his father, the "Great Mel," who, although a tailor by day, had cut a legendary social figure by night, but also the "Port" or dignity of his mother, whose severe respectability has kept the creditors from the shop's door and the business going.

Although this combination of traits eventually contributes to a mature self-respect in Evan, at first it poses a danger to his development. Both in external manners and in moral behavior Evan sees himself as misplaced. Unlike his father and his sister, he is disturbed by his anomalous position. The "Great Mel" had been a character of epic proportions, bridging the gap between the classes by the sheer force of his personality; the countess immerses herself in her campaign for social recognition with a complete conviction of merit—only Evan sees his position as "false." At the same time, from the moment he rides to his father's funeral in a coach he cannot afford, he betrays a strong element of pride: "Pride was the one developed faculty of Evan's nature. The Fates who mold us, always work from the mainspring" (63–64). And when pride gets the upper hand—when he unnecessarily insists on his tailor's background, when he equivocates or takes the countess's forgery on himself from a false sense of honor—it stands in the way of his real happiness and almost destroys Rose's as well.

Evan is one of Meredith's sentimentalists; he is infatuated with gentility and shrinks from such sordid concerns as money. But fortunately he learns: seeing the gentry at close range, he starts to distinguish between true nobility and sham and thus avoids becoming a complete snob like his sister. He also has the basically unspoilt, forthright Rose as his guide. Rose herself has to learn; in her early contempt of "snips" she betrays the thoughtlessness of an inexperienced young person. But she has an excellent model in her mother, Lady Jocelyn, who, because she herself comes from "trade," judges people fairly. Equally important, she has met Evan abroad, where he could shine on his own merits.

On the whole, Meredith draws a rather negative picture of the upper class, which has led Marxist critics to assert that he indicts the English class system and advocates a radical democracy.[17] The men of the Jocelyn circle are complacent, thoughtless, and brutally contemptuous of climbing outsiders; no wonder that Evan feels morally superior to them. Therefore, the end of the novel may seem, at first glance, inconsistent with its general tenor. Evan, one might assume, should have stayed with tailordom, with Rose, perhaps, as a devoted business manager like her mother-in-law. The all-round happy end may seem a sentimental concession to conventional reading taste, with the Cogglesby benevolence as a Dickensian deus ex machina. But Meredith makes obvious from the start that Evan's interests and strengths are appropriate to an upper-class profession: he would have made a wretched tailor.

It is true that Meredith humorously suggests an elevated view of the tailor's profession that recalls Carlyle's *Sartor Resartus*.[18] A tailor sees man divested of his external trappings; while he supplies society's distinguishing insignia, his penetrating view knows the underlying truth. To some degree Evan has to learn this aspect of the tailor's role, with particular attention to himself, since he is obviously over-impressed with the trappings of genteel life. Meredith, however, does not subscribe to the radical republicanism that sees men not only as equal in rights but also alike in qualities. Differences of gifts and tastes exist and have value. The master tailor who instructs Evan may have his humanizing hobbies, but he represents tailordom at its most dreary. Mrs. Mel Harrington gains Lady Jocelyn's respect through her sense of duty, but her plans for Evan are distressingly narrow. It is fair to say that Meredith draws a more sympathetic picture of his lower-class people than of most of the gentry. Yet his finest upper-class character, Lady Jocelyn, equals the common folk in plain good sense and surpasses them in fairness and sensitivity to the feelings of others. She most clearly fits John Cardinal Newman's definition of the gentleman as one who never inflicts pain.[19]

Of the three main characters, the countess is the most comically effective, one of Meredith's greatest creations. As one realizes early, she is utterly vulgar in her snobbery, but her single-mindedness also makes her a fascinating artist. Like the novelist himself, she refashions the world; lies and inventions, threats and insinuations take on reality when she weaves them strategically into the social fabric. Several times she overplays her hand, and the reader notes the desperateness of her schemes. Yet because she is completely convinced of her right to social preeminence, she manages to turn even her defeats into victories of a sort. Like Lady Blandish in *Richard Feverel,* she has the last word in the novel. Writing from her new field of action, Rome, after her rather dubious successes in England—she *has* brought Evan and Rose together, but not been able to conceal the tailor—she outlines further strategies for social eminence. Her astonishing "insight" that only Catholics can be gentlemen caps a brilliant career in snobbery and proves the inexhaustible vitality of human folly.

Sandra Belloni

Sandra Belloni (1864), originally called *Emilia in England,* is a sprawling, innovative novel held together by a central idea and a few threads of a complicated plot. The idea—the pernicious effect of sentimentalism on personal and social development—is a variation of Meredith's earlier themes and is dramatized by characters and character groupings somewhat similar to those of his two former novels.

The complex plot, however, is new and not entirely successful. It involves three different narrative strands and two narrative personae—a complication of perspective demanding, even more than in *Richard Feverel,* the intellectual involvement of the reader.

Emilia Alessandra Belloni, a beautiful half-Italian girl with a fine, though untrained voice, is "adopted" by the three daughters of a merchant, Samuel Pole. For the Pole sisters, she represents an object of interest by which they hope to attract a distinguished social circle. Their brother, Wilfrid, however, falls in love with her, wavering between her and Lady Charlotte, an older woman who offers an advantageous marriage. Emilia, considering herself engaged to Wilfrid, renounces her plan to study at the conservatory in Milan—a plan strongly promoted by the Greek millionaire and music lover Antonio Pericles, Mr. Pole's business partner. When she finds herself deserted by her lover, she temporarily loses her voice and with that, her patron, Mr. Pericles. From her desperate wanderings in London she is rescued by Merthyr Powys, a Welshman devoted to her beloved Italy. Under his guidance she recovers a sense of self-worth and breaks away from Wilfrid. Her voice returns, so that she can go to Italy to study, after all. Her story closes with a vague hint that a marriage with Merthyr may be in the future.

Wilfrid's dallying with both Emilia and Lady Charlotte has not only a sentimental but also a practical cause: his father, in desperate financial trouble, wishes him to make a profitable alliance. The second narrative strand of the novel traces the downfall of the Pole family: Mr. Pole's frantic attempt to marry an amorous Irish widow, whose funds he has mismanaged; the Pole daughters' violent opposition to this woman, whose vulgarity offends their sensibilities; and Mr. Pericles's anger at Wilfrid's dalliance with Emilia and his threat to expose Pole's financial ruin. When Pole's health gives way, his daughters, in order to save his life, have to equivocate and play along with the amorous widow's intentions. In the end it is Emilia who rescues the family from complete disgrace: in return for committing herself to her musical studies she exacts Mr. Pericles's promise of financial support and protection for the Poles.

Much of this narrative is farcical, since the Irish widow's vulgarity and stupidity play a large part in the Poles' predicament. However, in a subsidiary plot, Meredith comes close to a tragic view. Cornelia Pole, the most sentimental daughter, befriends Purcell Barrett, an impecunious young baronet, with whom she exchanges lofty sentiments. The two fall in love, but each one has too ideal a picture of the other, and too little sense of the reality of each other's feelings, to pursue their happiness. Believing himself to be rejected, Purcell shoots himself.

"So it is when you play at life," comments the narrator on this episode (266). The remark applies to all plots in the novel. The Pole sisters and Wilfrid "play at life" as true sentimentalists: they disregard the "immense debtorship for a thing done." Their sentimentalism shows itself in an exaggerated aesthetic pose. Ugly topics, such as money and marriage, are taboo in the girls' circle; true to Meredith's law of nature, these suppressed topics reassert themselves and control the Poles' lives. For Cornelia, the most "spiritual" of the trio, even love is too earthy; a soulful friendship is all she can admit. Whatever Cornelia feels and does is part of an aesthetic affectation denying her an honest commitment to another person. Since her lover is as fond of "fine Shades" and "nice Feelings" as she is and has put her on a pedestal of aesthetic veneration, the two engage in specious, highly evasive dialogue designed not to disturb the ideal concept each has of each other and—more important—of himself. The easiest way to avoid a commitment to reality is to speak in general terms—"devotedness to a father," "a child's first duty"—thus preserving, through the indisputable "beauty of sentiment," one's self-esteem and casting the urgency of one's partner into the light of vulgarity.

Purcell Barrett, whose morbid view of life is at one point explicitly contrasted with Emilia's (and thereby ironically exposed in its sentimentalism), is only a minor figure, but Meredith analyzes him with particular sensitivity. He gives him the background of an unhappy childhood, which overshadows a character with many admirable qualities and makes him prone to pessimism. As in *Richard Feverel* and, to some degree, *Evan Harrington,* parental failures play a large part in the disasters the protagonists incur in *Sandra Belloni;* Mr. Pole, the opportunistic businessman intimidated by his equally ruthless but more sophisticated daughters, is clearly as much at fault for the conduct of the Pole girls as the elder Sir Purcell for his son's lack of vital willpower. But native pride, family background, and circumstances all come together to effect a downfall for the Poles and Purcell Barrett which Emilia, with an equally unpromising background, is spared. In the young baronet Meredith traces the mesh of character and fate to its most bitter end. His pessimism, first challenged and then brutally confirmed by the impossible, "remorselessly reverential" expectations his love places on Cornelia, leads him to give up all attempts at self-assertion. The "Fates" even bring about his suicide, since he does not know—and declines to check—whether the pistol he takes on his last meeting is the one he has loaded. In his yielding to the "Fates" he resembles Sir Austin and Richard Feverel; his belief that he is destined for a special life of suffering incapacitates him when he is confronted with the actual "ordeal"—making the most of real life.

Emilia has almost nothing of Purcell's destructive self-consciousness. As another type of artist she is the healthy counterpart of his sentimental morbidity. Meredith contrasts her more directly and comically with the Pole girls—"our English sentimental, socially-aspiring damsels" versus "a girl of simplicity and passion" (*Letters,* 1:236). Emilia is a singer like the skylark: she sings because it is part of her nature. But in spite of her art, she never loses sight of mundane reality. When the Pole girls ask if the romantic forest setting inspires her, she replies that she has to sing outdoors in order not to disturb her housemates. Her artlessness brings out, by comic contrast, the ridiculous artificiality of their sentiments. She is also the touchstone to reveal the limitations and promises of Wilfrid, who is, like his sisters, initially captivated by the romance of the undiscovered artist, but then upset and challenged by the reality of her love. She does not play at life.

Meredith's sympathies are so overtly with Emilia throughout the novel that he can be accused of the very sentimentality he derides.[20] From the beginning she is his "epic" person, full of pleasure in life and healthy in taking what she needs for physical and spiritual sustenance. But the one year the novel spans shows a marked development in her. In the beginning she lets things happen to her. Renouncing her art for Wilfrid is her version of sentimental behavior, symbolized by her subsequent loss of voice. As in many Victorian novels the turning point comes with a kind of death and slow rebirth. For Emilia it means the discovery of her potentialities, specifically that she is still lovable. She becomes sophisticated: when she gathers her friends and enemies to demonstrate the return of her voice before her departure for the Italian conservatory, she orchestrates the meeting to display her social dexterity, which puts her on an equal level with her former rival for Wilfrid. Significantly, this meeting takes place in the woods, like the first encounter with the Poles, but now on a natural stage instead of in a mere wilderness. A stage is the place for her to be, and her new self-awareness ("What am I? I am a raw girl. I com-

mand nothing but raw and flighty hearts of men" [2:310]) and pur-
posefulness promise well for her career.

Wilfrid's development is less clear. Meredith's analysis of his behavior is consistently satiric; despite his disclaimer, the young man
comes across as both a coxcomb and a fool. Although he is no intellectual, he shares his sisters' love for "fine Shades" and "nice Feelings," as his concept of the ideal woman shows: "In his soul he adored
the extreme refinement of woman, even up to the thin edge of inanity. . . . Nothing was too white, too saintly, or too misty, for his
conception of abstract woman" (1:84). Clearly, Emilia does not fit
this ideal; on the other hand, her devotion flatters him immensely.
So he refashions her image to his satisfaction—the brilliant opera
singer who sings for him alone—leaving out, with some effort, what
jars his sensibilities. In this refashioning he does not take the real
Emilia into consideration and is constantly bewildered by the irrepressible impact of her personality. Meredith finds the roots of this
bewilderment in Wilfrid's lack of balance between blood and brain.
He is a "double man," composed of contradictory impulses pulling
him alternately to Lady Charlotte, who appeals to his brain, and Emilia, whose appeal to his blood he sentimentally conceals from himself.
Predictably, once he is firmly engaged to the lady, his suppressed instincts run wild. In his mad rush back to Emilia to gratify his senses,
he rides "the Hippogriff"—a Meredithian image for unrestrained behavior contrasting with true passion ("noble strength on fire"), which
is never quite divorced from common sense. Emilia is truly passionate; Wilfrid canters after her, literally and metaphorically, on his
"Hippogriff," but till the very end remains the "double man": "He
flung himself on a wayside bank, grovelling, to rise again calm and
quite ready for society, upon the proper application of the clothes-
brush" (2:290–291).

The "doubleness" of Wilfrid's nature appears again, on a much
larger scale, in the double perspective of the novel as a whole. The
narrative is shared by the Novelist, who actually tells the story, and
the Philosopher, who comments upon it. The Novelist is concerned
with the story itself and how it will sell; he has a conventional audience in mind and allows the Philosopher to interrupt him only as a
concession to "that acute and honourable minority which consents to
be thwacked with aphorisms and sentences and a fantastic delivery of
the verities" (2:230). This remark, obviously, is at the heart of Meredith's reader-directed irony. Who would not like to belong to an

acute and honorable minority that, by definition, rises above the need for sustained illusion and simple entertainment? To be thwacked with a fantastic delivery of the verities carries a great deal more prestige than to read a straightforward story—so Meredith ironically insinuates. This irony turns against the reader, revealing the honorable minority's own predilection for "fine Shades and nice Feelings." Meredith is having it both ways here: he wants a perceptive audience, but he derides one that prides itself on its perceptiveness. And he delights in thwacking us with aphorisms, but perceives the artificiality of doing so. In *Richard Feverel* Sir Austin and Adrian impress their audiences with verbal wit; in *Sandra Belloni,* so does the Philosopher. And shortly before the end of the novel, Meredith makes even clearer the ambivalence with which he regards the "philosophical" approach: the Novelist laughs the Philosopher off the stage. Witty metaphors— so this dismissal suggests—are artistic self-indulgences quite as sentimental as Cornelia's and Purcell's noncommittal gems of dialogue.[21] In fact, Meredith applies an additional turn to the irony he exploits. Sentimentalists, he argues, are important for civilization; even the Philosopher depends on them: "For if sentiment which spurns gold is the child of gold, so the fantastic philosopher who anatomizes Sentiment could not exist without Sentiment, wherefore let him be kindly cruel" (1:214–15). Under Meredith's scrutiny, sentimentalists, philosophers, creators of aphorisms, and acute minorities of readers are all shown to need the "kindly cruel" education of comedy.

Rhoda Fleming and *Vittoria*

Following *Sandra Belloni* Meredith published two minor novels on which he had been at work concurrently. *Rhoda Fleming* appeared in 1865; a shorter version of it has been identified by Lionel Stevenson in a story Meredith contributed to *Once a Week* in February 1861.[22] *Vittoria* (1867; serialized January-December 1866 in the *Fortnightly Review*) was a sequel to *Sandra Belloni,* planned while Meredith was writing the earlier novel, as the Novelist's announcement toward the end of the book makes clear (2:186). Both novels stand apart from the Meredith canon, and both are seriously flawed. Meredith was eager to improve his financial affairs at this time, having recently married again, and he courted popularity with the reading public by trying his hand at the novel of social reform and the historical novel. Neither of them was congenial to Meredith's temperament, although his other works amply prove his concern with social issues and his interest in the implications of history for the present. Consequently, neither of the two novels has been regarded very highly by the critics, then or now, and neither became a financial success.

Rhoda Fleming.   *Rhoda Fleming* treats the theme of the fallen woman and the difficulty of her social and spiritual recovery—a theme dramatized by Sir Walter Scott in *The Heart of Midlothian* and George Eliot in *Adam Bede*. Meredith couples this issue with those of economic exploitation and, implicitly, class warfare. Both upper and lower classes are shown at their meanest, but because many of the main characters, particularly in the lower class, are not clearly developed, the picture remains sketchy and unconvincing. Here Meredith's basic lack of contact with the English peasantry shows itself as a distinct handicap; in his treatment of rural life—for example, of meals at the farm—he can be arch and tediously long-winded, and his portrayal of the male rural protagonist, Robert Armstrong, is, at times, downright condescending.

Rhoda and Dahlia Fleming are daughters of a poor Kentish farmer, yearning for the attractions of London. Through an uncle, Dahlia is able to leave their bleak home for the city. She is seduced by Edward Blancove, the worldly son of a bank owner, who takes her to the Continent but, upon their return, deserts her, moving back into his own circle. Ashamed because she is not married, Dahlia evades her puritanically stern family. When she is finally discovered, with the help of Robert Armstrong, Rhoda Fleming's suitor, she is about to be married to Nic Sedgett, a ruffian in Edward's employ. The Flemings are relieved that Dahlia will acquire an honest name; Rhoda, particularly, pushes her into a marriage extremely repugnant to her sister. Edward's repentance of his callous behavior comes too late. Although Dahlia survives a suicide attempt and her marriage to Nic is found to be invalid, she has lost her capacity for happiness and lives, a saint of forgiveness, with Rhoda and Robert Armstrong till her early death. A subplot shows the Flemings' uncle abusing his trusted position at the bank and ending in a sad confusion of mind.

A major problem in this novel, particularly for a psychological writer like Meredith, is the fact that the lower-class characters are not very articulate. Dahlia Fleming, associated throughout with flower imagery, comes across as incredibly naive, colorless, and debilitated by her suffering. Meredith's making her a saint seems contrived and literary; saints are not usually marked by psychic exhaustion. Rhoda, the dark sister, is a fanatic character who suppresses feelings of sexual inadequacy and jealousy: her puritanical fervor to restore her sister's honor has a very ambiguous flavor, and her peculiar love-hate relationship with Robert reveals sexual frigidity coupled with a strong talent for manipulation. With his interest in psychological complexity Meredith could have done a great deal with this character; as it is, she is unusually static for a titular heroine as well as peripheral: for long stretches the reader sees very little of her.

Most of the novel concerns the two main male characters, Robert Armstrong and Edward Blancove. Robert is the good, simple rustic. He has redeemed his dissipated past through disciplined service, is friends with a gentleman, and farms on modern principles. But he is also moody, inarticulate, and potentially violent. His heedless and pointless exercise in brutality while trying to get hold of Blancove merely makes him look ridiculous and vulnerable to manipulation by his social superiors. A spiritual purification is suggested in his meeting with the suffering Dahlia. He becomes deeply sympathetic to "poor girls." In addition, his own love for Rhoda makes him somewhat understanding of the penitent Edward. But because of his inarticulateness and because Meredith analyzes him very little, his inner development is not convincing.

Meredith is more successful with the upper-class protagonist, Edward Blancove, a more intelligent and purposeful version of Wilfrid Pole. Training for the law and rhetorically gifted, Edward can persuade himself and others that his actions are motivated by a desire for general justice. Meredith, like George Eliot in *Adam Bede,* remarks that acts, not motivations, are crucial to social life: "Our deathlessness is in what we do, not in what we are. Comfortable youth thinks otherwise."[23] Edward's intentions toward Dahlia are kind enough, even after he has—inevitably—tired of her. But he is a Meredithian sentimentalist, whose verbal eloquence conceals moral cowardice and whose sophistry (he makes even Dahlia look guilty and in need of *his* forgiveness) anticipates the more fantastical mental gymnastics of later protagonists such as Sir Willoughby Patterne and Victor Radnor.

The motif of the fallen woman implies the idea that the sinner is morally superior to the seemingly righteous. This holds true for *Rhoda Fleming* in that Dahlia emerges as the one unblemished character. In the larger context, where the woman usually represents and is part of the exploited lower class, Meredith's novel blurs the issue. In both classes exploitation and greed appear everywhere. Farmer Fleming is quite as ready to sell Rhoda to a wealthy lover as Mrs. Lovett, a widow with a passion for gambling, is willing to renounce a deserving but poor man for a loveless but financially profitable marriage. Meredith shows a mercenary world, in which sex, beauty, and honor are bought and sold like market commodities and in which puritanical rigor and social callousness conspire in the disregard of innate human values.

Confrontations between the upper and lower classes do occur but are blunted through rhetorical manipulation and charm by the gentry and the obtuseness and deference of the peasantry. Farmer Fleming manages even to see an affinity between himself and Squire Blancove: both, he asserts, are wronged fathers who should not be blamed for the sins of their offspring. That his argument is wrong in more than one sense illustrates the ambiguous and deceptive character of social relations as well as of moral attitudes in *Rhoda Fleming*. As David Howard has shown, failures of understanding, failures of unambiguous moral development, failures even of conclusive action mark the novel throughout.[24] These failures also occur as flaws in the narrative structure of *Rhoda Fleming;* the evasions, instances of vagueness, and peripheralism that make the novel so irritating unintentionally confirm Meredith's ambivalent attitude about the possibility of social communication.

Vittoria. *Vittoria* grew out of Meredith's disenchantment with the petty and morbid people he had portrayed in *Sandra Belloni* and his wish to write "epic" fiction.[25] Italy in its protracted war of independence, which captured the sympathies and imagination of countless European intellectuals during the nineteenth century, offered the appropriate subject matter. In *Sandra Belloni* the uprisings of the 1840s are shown to stir Emilia's passionate patriotism. Toward the end of the book the Novelist, announcing Emilia's departure for Italy and the sequel to her story in another volume, explains Meredith's anticipated change of narrative stance. In England, he asserts, a complacent society has allowed the growth of petty vices calling for chastisement by the Philosopher (the ironic placing of the Philosopher notwithstanding). In Italy events are drawn on a larger scale, and the passions they arouse are no longer the object of comic scrutiny; thus, the new novel lacks the Philosopher. *Vittoria* has almost no authorial irony. The irony that does appear results from the events of the plot bearing upon characters in unexpected ways.

Meredith tries to dramatize the idea that personal and national destinies may run parallel, informing each other and growing according to similar laws. Individual fates receive a measure of dignity from their link with the fate of the country, and the frustrations, sufferings, and victories of the country reflect the moral weaknesses and triumphs of its individual citizens.[26]

The novel covers the early stages of the struggle for independence, 1848–49. It takes place mostly in Milan, a hotbed of nationalism and a center of conflicting interests. Meredith, however, also moves the protagonists around from one location to another in order to bring them close to the most important historical events; at times, plot serves only as a passport to scenes of historical interest, which Meredith knew well from his assignment as a war reporter during the Italian-Austrian War of 1866. The novel poses not only geographical and historical problems for the reader; it also presents a bewildering network of narrative strands. Emilia, the heroine of *Sandra Belloni*, who now calls herself Vittoria Campa, nominally holds the plot together, and all major characters are shown in their response to her, but she is often peripherally or not at all on the scene, while conspiracies, plots, and counterplots involve, altogether, more than a hundred major and minor figures.

To help the reader through this welter of incidents and to stress, from the start, the correspondence between personal and national destinies, Meredith provides an extended synopsis of an opera Vittoria sings at La Scala. The opera pits a pair of lovers against the intrigues of a ruler and his daughter; the daughter temporarily separates the couple, but in the end they are reunited, though the heroine dies at her rival's hand. The plot is a transparent allegory of the Italian condition: Austrian intrigue temporarily divides monarchist and republican Italy and suppresses the independence movement, but cannot quench its spirit. Like the opera, the novel depicts—through the estrangement, reconciliation, and suffering of Vittoria and her aristocratic fiancé, Carlo Ammiani—the course of the revolution to its defeat, with the promise of ultimate triumph.

Vittoria is the only woman among a group of nationalists planning the 1848 uprising. At her La Scala debut she sings an inflammatory aria, galvanizing the audience and putting herself in danger of arrest by the Austrian occupiers. She is whisked away by her friends, but not before she has engaged herself to Carlo Ammiani, a nobleman who combines fiery patriotism with personal vanity and impetuosity. En route to safety in Meran, Vittoria helps a notorious conspirator escape from the Austrians, making use of her former lover, Wilfrid Pole, who now serves in the Austrian army, and bitterly antagonizing two noble Austrian ladies, the Lenkensteins. While Carlo is imprisoned in Milan, Vittoria moves to Turin, supporting the Italian cause through her singing. Her admiration of the Sardinian king, whom the Milanese despise, leads to an estrangement with her fiancé deepened by the machinations of an opportunistic noblewoman, Violetta d'Isorella, who appeals to Carlo's vanity. Vittoria's reluctance to join Carlo's mother and await their marriage in safety does not alleviate their estrangement, but eventually they are married and have a few months of happiness together, overshadowed only by Carlo's traditional prejudice against women as political participants. After the king's defeat at Novara, Carlo feels himself bound to carry on the fight, although he knows he has been betrayed and his enterprise is hopeless. He and his few comrades fall; Vittoria resists despair for the sake of her unborn child. An epilogue shows her celebrating Italian freedom in 1859 with her son.

Vittoria attempts to illustrate the psychology of the revolution through the psychology of its participants. Vittoria and Carlo represent its essential nobility of purpose but also its immaturity. Along with their devotion to the cause they show conflicting impulses and attitudes, such as his pride, arrogance, and chauvinism and her abdication of will, which reduce the effectiveness of their actions. The other participants in the movement are also variously in conflict. Oppositions and alliances are drawn all across society; Austrians and Italians are not only enemies but also, occasionally, friends, relatives, or lovers. Among the Italians, republicans and aristocrats mistrust and scheme against one another; artistic and sexual links and rivalries further complicate the picture. Political considerations are, on the whole, subordinate to pride, suspicion, and revenge but also affected by loyalty, personal fondness, and class allegiances transcending national lines.

Although Meredith's sympathies are with the Italians because he believes that historical evolution favors a nation committed to its liberty, he nevertheless draws Italians and Austrians impartially. He acknowledges the military prowess and honorable intentions of the occupiers and suggests that the Italians, despite individual bravery, are not yet ready for nationhood because of their many disparate and conflicting interests. In the conduct of individuals Meredith attempts to convey the ambiguity and variableness of motivations, but because of the preponderance of plot in the novel, analysis is often sketchy. Both Carlo and Vittoria do not come to life until fairly late in the story, when their relationship is tested not so much by the demands of the revolution as by the strains of personal prejudices and obsolete social conventions.

Vittoria comes closer than any other Meredith novel to the "blood and glory" type he derides in contemporary fiction. It is crowded with incident: conspiracies, abductions, duels, attempted murders, escapes, executions, and imprisonments mark the plot. The reader is often bewildered by mistaken identities and half-revealed secrets. Adding to the difficulty are Meredith's self-acknowledged habit of accounting for each character's motivations and an allusive style in the dialogues of the aristocracy and the plotters. The technical problems of the novel undeniably reduce one's reading pleasure. Geraldine Jewsbury, an early critic, undoubtedly spoke for many when she called *Vittoria* "unmerciful."[27] Another reviewer described it as "Mr. Meredith's very clever, though rather unreadable, performance."[28] While acknowledging the ambitiousness of its aim, the magnitude of its design, and the generosity of its spirit, a modern reader can only agree with these verdicts. Meredith himself recognized the novel's deficiencies and, in *Harry Richmond,* turned its strengths to better account.[29]

Chapter Four

Novels of the Seventies and Eighties: "An Embrace of Contrasts"

From 1871 until 1885 Meredith published five novels and three novellas; he also wrote an important essay on comedy, numerous poems, an incomplete play—*The Satirist*—and scenes of another play, *The Sentimentalists*.[1] In these years of strenuous and often less than confident work, he reached the stature of a major author. Both artistically and financially, he became successful, although he clung to his self-image of the misunderstood and unappreciated writer and continued to use it for ironic purposes in his work.

The novels of this period are solid achievements, but they also show, more clearly than the earlier ones, the tensions out of which his art arises. Meredith moves away from the strikingly autobiographical matter evident in *Richard Feverel* and *Evan Harrington* without giving up his intense concern with sexual and class relations. At the same time he traces more and more minutely the complex psychological development of individuals—their self-delusions, vacillations, momentary insights, and impulsive resolutions. As he tried to do less successfully in *Sandra Belloni,* he indicates that individual shortcomings and general flaws in the social structure spring from identical sources and have comparable results. To dramatize this idea he makes his protagonists more prominent people than in his earlier novels. Two of them, Beauchamp and Dr. Alvan, are politically active; Sir Willoughby is the leading figure of his county; Harry Richmond not only stands for a parliamentary election but is also the prospective fiancé of a German princess and—possibly—a descendant of royalty; and Diana Warwick, an author and a celebrated hostess, takes a lively interest in political issues. The delusions and self-contradictions of these characters are related to the shortcomings Meredith sees in the England of his time, particularly to its complacency, its resistance to change, and its hypocritical attitude toward women. His protagonists see themselves as social, political, or cultural leaders, thus allowing Meredith to comment extensively on England's weaknesses in all areas of public life. But his main concern continues to be the history of individuals, which he traces with ironic emphasis on the futility of their intentions in the public sphere.

The protagonists of the middle novels are developed from recognizable predecessors. Harry Richmond's struggle to reconcile his opposing responsibilities points back to Evan Harrington. Nevil Beauchamp's heroism recalls Richard Feverel's fatuous idealism. Sir Willoughby's arrogant egoism is prefigured in Sir Austin Feverel's desire to control his son's life, and his misanthropy in the sentimental posturing of Cornelia Pole and Purcell Barrett, who also anticipate the "tragic comedians" Alvan and Clothilde in their misconception of each other. Finally, Sandra Belloni's and Dahlia Fleming's problems as artist and woman, respectively, come together in the ordeal of Diana Warwick. In each case, the later protagonist is more complex and sophisticated than his or her predecessor, and to show the development of such personalities convincingly, Meredith exerts greater control over his plots than before. He curbs his tendency toward subsidiary plots and expressly avoids "palpable climaxes"—not only melodramatic or sensational exposures, but also sudden, unexplained leaps of insight that bring about instant radical conversions. His method leads to anticlimactic conclusions: marriages that will be satisfying but not glamorous, or deaths without the tragic splendor of self-knowledge. "Banality, thy name is marriage," says Diana Warwick shortly before engaging herself to the suitable but unexciting Tom Redworth. Her friend Emma Dunstane, Meredith's spokesman throughout the novel, replies, "Your business is to accept life as we have it,"[2] and this determined sobriety reflects Meredith's artistic as well as philosophical stance. His attitude aims at the high indifference of Nature herself, to whom marriage is part of the business of life and death the indisputable end of it.

The novels of Meredith's middle period move steadily from external to internal history, from a preponderance of romance and action to psychological analysis. However, in the seventies and early eighties Meredith was also particularly interested in the nature and function of comedy, and some of his novellas as well as his most renowned novel, *The Egoist,* resulted from his attempts to write "internal history" in comic terms. (*Evan Harrington* had been an earlier effort.)

Meredith set down his concept of comedy in his only sustained piece of literary theory, the lecture "On the Idea of Comedy and the Uses of the Comic Spirit," published in the *New Quarterly Magazine,* April 1877. In its thesis, its underlying assumptions, and its implicit self-contradictions, the *Essay on Comedy,* as it is customarily called, offers the key to the artistic goals and problems of Meredith's middle period.

Comedy, Meredith states, is rooted in civilization and cannot exist without "a society of cultivated men and women . . . wherein ideas are current and the perceptions quick."[3] It addresses the intellect "with reference to the operations of the social world upon their characters" (80) and is intimately connected with common sense in the double meaning of reasonableness and a spirit of community. That all civilizations are founded in common sense is, for Meredith, an incontrovertible fact. They protect themselves from self-destruction and decay through the Comic Spirit, a "vigilant sense of a collective supervision" guarding against excesses of folly. The ideal Meredithian society bases its conduct on a "bright and positive, clear Hellenic perception of facts" (63)—one recalls the Apollonian spirit in his poetry and his insistence on the realism of the greatest writers—and turns the weapon of comedy against folly, "the daughter of Unreason and Sentimentalism." (57)

The spirit of comedy is the enemy of anything pretentious, overblown, hypocritical, and pedantic. Though it does not attack the natural conditions beyond the control of man's reason, it is merciless in its pursuit of anything offending sound sense and fair justice: "For folly is the natural prey of the Comic and it is with the springing delight of hawk over heron, hound after fox, that it gives her chase, never fretting, never tiring, sure of having her, allowing no rest" (56). The imagery of this passage suggests evolutionary processes; comedy, Meredith implies, serves Nature in speeding the advance of the human race.

Prompted by his historical and ethnological interests, Meredith devotes a large part of the *Essay* to a survey of national literatures intended to show how much room they give to comedy. England, he asserts, has had few great comic writers. Although the English esteem common sense, their taste, limited by a prudish sense of propriety, runs to broad, sentimental, occasionally farcical humor or to sharp satire. Both sentimental humor and satire disregard the full reality of human nature, but of the two, Meredith finds satire the more objectionable since it is not founded in sympathy and claims a superior status for the critic of society. This claim, brilliantly dramatized in Molière's Alceste, is most vulnerable to the shafts of the Comic Spirit: if the comic writer lacks a profound sense of communality, he himself becomes an object of laughter. True comedy, in contrast to satire ("a blow in the back or the face") and irony, which is satire concealed in ambiguity, maintains benevolence and perfect politeness in its attack. Its laughter is thoughtful but never bitter; its attitude is "humanely malign."

Meredith's use of the terms *satire, irony,* and *comedy* is not systematic and differs from today's usage. According to the *Essay,* he rejects irony, but the distance he maintains from his narrative material we would normally call ironic. To him *satire* suggests *cynicism,* a term he does not use in the *Essay.* In his novels *comedy* spans all variations from farce and moist-eyed humor to hard-hitting satire, particularly in his comments on contemporary politics and social mores. The *Essay* should be seen as an expression of Meredith's artistic ideals and intentions rather than as the definitive statement about his work for which it is often taken. The "volleys of silvery laughter" sounding through his novels are often accompanied by peripheral noise, either the clucking over a favorite character or the hiss of barely concealed hostility over those who too blatantly offend reason.

Even within the *Essay* Meredith concedes that "Life, we know too well, is not a comedy, but something strangely mixed" (26); no character, however foolish, is circumscribed by his folly alone. To deny him a certain dignity of motivation and pathos of erring makes the comic writer himself guilty of exaggeration and "shapelessness." Through various methods—shifts in perspective, expansions and constrictions of focus, and a constant play of metaphor—Meredith attempts to do justice to the double role comedy demands of the writer who also aims to be true to life.

Meredith's enthusiastic praise of Molière in the *Essay* makes it seem that he took the French neoclassical playwright as his literary guide. Actually, the novels of the middle period— with the partial exception of *The Egoist*—suggest a different model, also mentioned in the *Essay*: Cervantes. The Spanish writer has "an embrace of contrasts beyond the scope of the comic poet, . . . fusing the tragic sentiment with the comic narrative" (43–44). It is this embrace of contrasts that for Meredith constitutes the true presentation of life.[4]

Dorothy van Ghent has pointed out that one of the salient features in Cervantes's *Don Quixote* is the prevalence of paradox, "a concentrated opposition of two outlooks . . . both of which have to be held in the mind at once."[5] This is precisely what characterizes Meredith's middle and later novels. Paradox appears most obviously in the oxymoronic title *The Tragic Comedians* and the "epitaph" to *The Egoist*: "Through very love of self himself he slew." The second of these examples indicates a certain moral patness Meredith assumes in his particularly comic mode. He tempts the reader to record the moral of the story as a rather self-evident case of "self-destructive egoism." It is true, of course, that his novels can be read that way. But *egoism* is a highly complex term in Meredith's vocabulary, involving not only self-indulgence but also self-creation. His characters are not—normally—monsters of egoism, or even fixed personalities, but shifting, growing, self-contradictory, as his frequent metaphor of the divided person indicates. His comedy, always tied to man's ultimately futile attempt to create a stable, permanent identity and to establish irrefutably logical ground rules for living, does not conceal the tragedy inherent in this endeavor; Meredith's is comedy in the face of tragedy, and the very stridency of its assertion betrays its vulnerability. Meredith does not integrate the comic and the tragic modes but plays them off against each other. The shape of his novels is determined by this paradoxical vision, which manifests itself in the contradictions informing the protagonists' destinies.

The Adventures of Harry Richmond

Among Meredith's early novels, *Evan Harrington* had been his most straightforward comedy. He used many of the same themes and even went back to his family history for the first novel of his middle period, *The Adventures of Harry Richmond* (1871; serialized September 1870–November 1871 in the *Cornhill Magazine*). The work, however, is more complicated than *Evan Harrington;* it draws on the tradition of the bildungsroman, the picaresque novel,[6] and the romance in addition to the comedy of manners, and the use of a first-person narrator offers an interesting treatment of perspective reflecting the protagonist's maturation. In *Evan Harrington* satire and benevolence had been rather sharply split, benevolent humor embracing the protagonist, satire pursuing the adventurous Countess. In his growth from early childhood through marriage Harry Richmond is shown, through the "autobiographer's" voice, to work his way to a synthesis of the two attitudes, to achieve it in his understanding of his father and his somewhat sardonic acceptance of himself.

As a five-year-old, Harry Richmond is taken from his maternal grandfather's house by his father, Richmond Roy, a shiftless adventurer whose grandiose schemes for prosperity include a claim of royal ancestry. Although Richmond Roy alternates between profligacy and debtors' prison, eventually vanishing, apparently for good, from his son's life, he leaves an indelible impression of his charm and generosity on the child. After a few years at a boarding school Harry returns to his grandfather, Squire Beltham, a rich, prudent old man who detests his irresponsible son-in-law. Squire Beltham plans to make Harry heir to his estate if the boy will renounce his father and eventually marry Janet Ilchester, a young cousin and Beltham's favorite.

Harry, however, continues to seek for his father. Chance brings him to Germany, where he finds Richmond Roy as a court entertainer in a small principality. He also meets the beautiful princess Ottilia whom Roy is scheming to secure for him. Over the next few years Harry supports his father's plans, even though he gradually recognizes the weakness of Roy's character. Enchanted with the German princess, he wins her love, but her family resists, and Roy's intrigues to secure the match only compromise the young man. Father and son return to England, Harry with a sense of relief, Richmond Roy with even greater eagerness to bring about the marriage. Eventually he manages to bring the princess over to England on fraudulent grounds, but his attempt to blackmail her into marriage fails when her family, as well as Squire Beltham and Janet, protect her against this scheme. Harry himself is mortified by his father's unscrupulous behavior and relieved when the engagement comes to an end. Squire Beltham ferociously denounces Roy Richmond and disinherits Harry for his loyalty to the crushed adventurer. After Beltham's death, Harry and Janet, who has inherited the estate, are brought together through Princess Ottilia. At their homecoming after their wedding Richmond Roy perishes in a fire resulting from his plan to illuminate the manor in their honor.

This plot summary does not convey the abundance of adventures experienced by the protagonist. Particularly in the first half of the novel, the spirit of "anything can happen" is akin to that in *The Shaving of Shagpat:* as a child, Harry lives in a fairy-tale world in which only the present and an apparently limitless future count. The narrator—the grown-up Harry—evokes this world by withholding any explanatory or evaluating comment; the child's unquestioning acceptance of the unusual life he leads with his father comes to the reader with persuasive immediacy. With the boy's increasing self-awareness the narrator's voice becomes more analytical, pointing out delusions and referring to insights he has gained in the meantime. Toward the end his style occasionally approaches that of the usual Meredithian narrator, and he locates himself, with commendable modesty—and Meredithian self-directed irony—between the "happy bubbling fool" and the philosopher.

By withholding comment early in the story, the narrator allows us not only to experience the magic openness of childhood but also to identify it with the attractive figure of Richmond Roy. To his son, Roy is romance, full of love, promise, and limitless energy. He is a magician or a giant of fairy tales, a supernatural force. Characteristically, Richmond Roy himself boasts about his superhuman powers of energy and inventiveness. He also sees himself under the protection of his own dead mother; both in his blindness to the constraints of reality and in his refusal to make himself, rather than Providence, responsible for his life, he remains an unteachable child. It is essential for Harry's own maturity that he sever himself from this child-father, without rejecting romance itself as a source of life's beauty.

Like *Richard Feverel* the novel shows a son's need to understand himself by distancing himself from his father. But as in *Evan Harrington* the protagonist has inherited conflicting qualities he needs to reconcile. Richmond Roy, the unstable, always wandering "ship of cinnamon wood on a sea that rolled mighty, but smooth immense broad waves,"[7] whose conduct is a mixture of "fiery" determination and "airy" self-confidence, is contrasted with the "earthy" Squire Beltham. Together they represent qualities in Harry that must be brought into harmony. At first glance, his movement seems to be clearly from Richmond Roy to Squire Beltham. He outgrows his childhood fascination with the "magician" and is embarrassed by the adventurer. The fact that when he plays along with his father's schemes he feels uneasy and sordid shows his solid Beltham side. On the other hand, he cannot simply drop his father, who is, after all, his past. "We are the sons of yesterday, not of the morning" (1:339), comments the narrator; renouncing his father would make Harry guilty of the same irresponsibility marking Roy himself, whereas supporting him in his downfall shows him, paradoxically, with a sense of obligation characteristic of the Belthams.

The battle between Richmond Roy and Squire Beltham for Harry appears to be echoed in his wavering between the two women—the princess selected for him by his father and Janet, his grandfather's favorite. To both Harry and the reader, Ottilia seems to represent the apex of romance, the fairy-tale princess to whom the prince in disguise aspires. She is, as Gillian Beer has observed, a supreme instance of a romantic cliché translated into narrative fact.[8] The point Harry has to learn—and Richmond Roy refuses to—is that she *is* real, with obligations of her own and undeniable expectations of her lover. Though she loves Harry, she refuses to be manipulated like a puppet princess in Roy's fantasy world. In fact, it is she, not the Providence Roy invokes, who arranges her fiancé's chance to stand for Parliament—a socially useful activity to weigh against the increasingly irresponsible, even anarchical plottings of his father.

Ottilia, Harry's guiding star, exerts a very real moral pressure on him. She is his "touchstone, a relentless mirror" (2:216). Janet's unimaginative sensibleness affects him differently: "I thought of Janet— she made me gasp for air; of Ottilia, and she made me long for earth" (2:233). The contrast is exaggerated, coming from his own divided nature and his inability to see either of them as they really are. Once he realizes that the real Ottilia, though attractive, is not right for him, but that Janet, with her capacity to be refined from "iron" into "finest steel," is his perfect mate, he gives up the futile distinction. Symbolically, Ottilia will remain the "home" of his highest ideals, but Janet gives him a home on earth.

Actually, the end does not work quite so neatly. For Riversley, the home Janet was to offer him, burns down. Metaphorically, the fire consuming both the Beltham inheritance and the deluded Richmond Roy in a self-destructive apotheosis images Harry's victory over the past divisions in himself. It also means a departure into uncertainty, a future in which neither the material privileges nor the fantastical schemes of the past will shelter him any longer. Through suffering and contact with a larger world Janet and Harry are no longer merely Beltham's heirs.

The theme of inheriting the past persists throughout the novel, as a counterpoint to the timelessness of romance embodied by Richmond Roy. It allows Meredith to examine critically what he considered a prominent flaw in the British national character: the unthinking adoption of past and, he implies, outworn ideologies and policies. The novel makes this point not only dramatically, showing Harry wasting his inheritance on his father's extravagant habits, but also explicitly through the comments by a foreign observer. Ottilia's teacher, a radical philosopher, finds Harry unsatisfactorily vague of purpose and harangues him on the indolence and lack of leadership among the British upper class. The professor's stridency is comical, but the points he makes are Meredith's, as his letters of the 1870s to Captain Maxse show.[9]

Such philosophical discussions are not part of the typical autobiographical English novel, but are frequently found in the German bildungsroman. Meredith's debt to Goethe, whom he acknowledged as one of the masters of realism, and to the archetypal bildungsroman, *Wilhelm Meister's Apprentice Years,* is evident throughout *Harry Richmond.* For example, the term "a beautiful soul" ("eine schöne Seele"), by which Ottilia is described, comes directly from the diary of a character in the German novel. Harry's choice between an idealistic and an eminently practical woman is anticipated in Wilhelm Meister's position between two equally contrasted female figures. And both the German and the English novel show a protagonist attracted excessively to romance but able to integrate it into a more realistic concept of life.[10] As a typical Englishman, Harry cannot be shown to enjoy philosophical speculation, but by placing him in a foreign environment that at first glance seems merely romantic but turns out to engage his mental and moral faculties, Meredith brings in philosophy by the back door. In addition, Meredith extends the scope of the bildungsroman because Harry's development takes place in a clearly defined social context: he stands for the British upper classes who should lead the nation; he shares their weaknesses and their modest promise. Harry's growth—his moral refinement as well as his mature appreciation of a limited but real sphere for social action—paradigmatically outlines Meredith's hopes for his age and his country.

Beauchamp's Career

Like *Harry Richmond, Beauchamp's Career* (1876; serialized August 1874–December 1875 in the *Fortnightly Review*) tells the history of a young man who finds his aspirations narrowly constrained by circumstances. The story allows Meredith to examine the conditions of nineteenth-century England through his protagonist's search for a

socially and personally rewarding career.[11] But *Beauchamp's Career* is a
very sober novel; romance, in the form of the hero's love for a Frenchwoman, and political idealism—the radicalism of Beauchamp's mentor, Dr. Shrapnel—are given little room in the fictional world,
although they fill a large part of Beauchamp's mind. The novel
stresses the futility and pathos rather than the vitality and joy of human endeavors.

On his return to England from a distinguished career in the Crimean War, Nevil Beauchamp, ardent patriot and political idealist,
stands for Parliament as a Radical—in contradiction to his Tory family's tradition. His uncle, the Honorable Everard Romfrey, denies his
support, giving it to a Tory cousin instead. A summons from a young
Frenchwoman, Renée de Croisnel, whom Nevil has unsuccessfully
courted, interrupts his campaign. His journey stirs up rumors about
a "French affair," damaging not only his political chances but also his
hopes of marrying Cecilia Halkett, an eminently suitable British heiress. Although Cecilia does not share Beauchamp's Radicalism, she
supports him against the trickeries of the Tory electioneers; but after
Renée appears in London in flight from her husband and offers herself
to Nevil, Cecilia's patience is exhausted and she engages herself to a
more reliable Tory suitor. Nevil, already compromised by Renée, has
to send her home.

His estrangement from his family is intensified through the brutal
horsewhipping Romfrey administers to Nevil's mentor, the aged Dr.
Shrapnel, after Shrapnel's purported slandering of Rosamund Culling,
a widow who acts as Romfrey's hostess. There has been no slander,
but Mrs. Culling, sharing Romfrey's anger at the influence Dr.
Shrapnel exerts on Nevil, hesitates to set the record straight. In his
obsessive desire to make his uncle apologize to the doctor, Nevil ne-
glects his political campaign. He loses decisively and subsequently
falls severely ill. His perilous state brings about a change in his relatives: Rosamund Culling, having become Lady Romfrey, regrets her
unfairness to Dr. Shrapnel and persuades her husband to apologize.
This restoration of the family honor helps Nevil recover. He marries
his devoted nurse, Jenny Denham, Dr. Shrapnel's niece, and settles
down to philosophy and family duties. The novel ends, however, with
Nevil's death by drowning while trying to save a slum child from the
river.

Beauchamp's life ends before it has shaped itself into any definite
career; the meaning it has acquired at its close has little to do with

his stated intentions, although his intentions carry extraordinary weight in determining his day-to-day conduct. Beauchamp lives by idealistic principles; the novel shows how ineffective and yet how necessary these principles are in the real world. *Beauchamp's Career* explores the possibility and perils of heroism in an ideological program that deliberately rejects heroic concepts and figures.

Beauchamp is a hero in the traditional sense—an excellent soldier who has saved several lives. Public admiration appears to offer a promising position from which to start a political career. However,

to be a public favorite is his last thought. Beauchampism, as one confronting him calls it, may be said to stand for nearly everything which is the obverse of Byronism, and rarely woos your sympathy, shuns the statuesque pathetic, or any kind of posturing. For Beauchamp will not even look at happiness to mourn its absence; melodious lamentations, demonical scorn, are quite alien to him. His faith is in working and fighting.[12]

Imitating this antimelodramatic stance, the narrator calls Beauchamp's story "artless" and "plotless." Meredith is, as many of his comments in his letters and fiction show, in sympathy with Beauchamp's simple faith in working and fighting. But he also sees the potential ludicrousness of adopting on principle an anti-Byronic stance. The novel shows Beauchamp overcome not only by England's stolid indifference to his Radical ideas but also by his uncompromising, even fanatical nature. The young man is in the grip of a paradox: the very qualities that have made him a hero in the first place—his courage, patriotism, personal integrity, and single-minded devotion to duty—militate against his success in political life because they alienate him from his less virtuous but more practical fellow citizens.

Meredith makes clear, partly through parody of the language of romance, that even the most dedicated "Beauchampism"—single-minded devotion to duty—does not preclude its own brand of egoism. In both the political and the personal spheres Beauchamp is marked by impetuosity and fanaticism and thus subject to the correction of the Comic Spirit. As a knight-errant championing the cause of women, the rights of the common man, a fair distribution of wealth, and a better military, he shows an often ludicrous lack of compromise, and his sense of priorities is debatable, as his reaction to the horsewhipping of Dr. Shrapnel shows. He tries to put into action the ideas of his mentor; but it is obvious to the reader that these ideas—expressed in Dr. Shrapnel's gusty "wind-of the-orchard" style reminiscent of Carlyle—are no practical blueprint for action, however spiritually elevating. Not that Dr. Shrapnel's messages are disapproved by Meredith; he merely mocks Nevil's single-mindedness in a country temperamentally opposed to political idealism and manageable chiefly through appeals to its self-interest.[13] Meredith also shows, however, that Nevil's personal integrity has an ennobling, though limited effect on those close to him; calling on his uncle to behave honorably toward a political opponent may not change the political lines, but it restores credibility to the aristocracy's code of fair play.

In his private life Beauchamp starts out as what Meredith considered a typical male egoist, both worshiping and condescending to the women of his circle. Although he is aware of complex questions about their situation in society, he chooses to ignore these issues, at least as far as concerns himself. Renée fascinates him because she embodies the romance of a foreign culture; in this respect she resembles Princess Ottilia in *Harry Richmond,* and Nevil, like Harry, tries to appropriate her for his own emotional gratification without considering that her charm is inseparable from her cultural background. With Cecilia he faces a somewhat similar dilemma: enchanted with her upper-class attractiveness—she strikes him as the epitome of the English lady, an object of immense decorative value—he still tries to convert her to Radicalism. To both women he vows unchanging devotion, but when devotion is required of him, he turns out to have changed. More important, so have they, under his unwitting influence. The novel, indeed, is full of misread signals and missed opportunities, which would be comical if Nevil, Renée, and Cecilia were not so appealing and so pathetically eager to do the right thing. Because of Nevil's fundamental blindness to his influence on the women he loves, both Renée and Cecilia end in loveless marriages, with a poignant awareness of the lost possibility of a larger life. More quixotic is the outcome of Rosamund Culling's love for Nevil: after she has married his uncle, largely to help return him to Romfrey's good graces, she realizes that the child she is about to bear will end Nevil's prospects of inheriting the Romfrey title and estate.

The end of the novel—Beauchamp's drowning—seems rather arbitrary at first glance.[14] Meredith insisted to his critics, though he gave no reason, that his hero had to die. What he may have had in mind was the fact that there was no other satisfactory way to cope with the paradox inherent in Beauchamp's anti-Byronic heroism. Had Beauchamp lived longer, he would have had to compromise to achieve even partial acceptance of his program, or else he would have become an ineffectual figure like Dr. Shrapnel. In either case the end would have been a negation of heroism in the traditional sense. And Meredith does make the point—implicitly—that individual heroic action in the uncompromising, headlong, and essentially private manner of the knight-errant is an ineffectual gesture in the modern world, which requires cooperation and compromise. Beauchamp's end is in keeping with his anti-Byronic stance, which anticipates a more democratic outlook without being temperamentally able to fully adopt it. After a futile, frustrated career, thwarted largely by his own limitations and in the end marked by a general resignation, his simple act reaffirms the essence of his heroism. Drowning during a rescue attempt is the ultimate anti-Byronic Beauchampism, a confirmation of values that cancels the hero's former isolation but annihilates him. Meredith leaves the reader not with a political commentary on the condition of England, or with a blueprint for reform, but with a simple metaphor for the paradox of self-affirmation through self-sacrifice.

The Egoist

In *The Egoist: A Comedy in Narrative* (1879; serialized June 1879–January 1880 in the *Glasgow Weekly Herald*), Meredith attempted to put fully into fiction the ideas he had expressed in his *Essay on Comedy*. Apart from the early *Evan Harrington, The Egoist* is, by his own definition, Meredith's only truly comic novel, and in technical control, psychological depth, and flexibility of language it shows the writer at the height of his craft. Meredith confessed, however, to Robert Louis Stevenson that only "half myself" was in it; once he had finished *The Egoist,* he turned away from the exclusively comic mode of writing with evident relief (*Letters,* 1:297). Indeed, even within *The Egoist* there are hints—in the form of authorial asides and metaphors—that Meredith was questioning the adequacy of comedy while he was, with dazzling virtuosity, employing its conventions.[15]

The Egoist approximates, as closely as prose narrative can, the stage comedy in which Molière had excelled. It adheres to the three unities of classical drama: the unity of time—its action spans only a few days; the unity of place—a single setting; and the unity of plot—there are no subsidiary plots. The novel contains a number of typical stage devices: mistaken identities, the hidden listener, and the assembling of all characters in the final scene. Chapter headings take the form of stage directions, and action advances mostly by dialogue. Meredith's skill in imitating conversational speech patterns, particularly ellipsis and a careless use of personal pronouns, serves him well in creating the comic complications of his drama.

The protagonist is Sir Willoughby Patterne of Patterne Hall. His fiancée, Clara Middleton, visits him with her father and in the course of a few days realizes that the idea of marrying him has become repugnant to her. He refuses to give her up, having been jilted once before. She tries to flee but returns on the advice of his sensible cousin Vernon Whitford. Willoughby's jealousy fastens on Colonel de Craye, his friend, with whom Clara has been seen returning. Still refusing to release Clara but afraid of the rumors starting to circulate, he tries to protect himself by also courting Laetitia Dale, a young woman of the neighborhood who has long adored him. The boy Crossjay, a houseguest, overhears Sir Willoughby proposing to Laetitia, a breach of faith that sets Clara free. But to spite de Craye and "punish" Clara, Sir Willoughby tries to bring about a union between Clara and Vernon, to their secret delight. In order to avoid the county's derision at a third jilting—for Laetitia has meanwhile lost her illusions about him—Willoughby must humble himself and accept this lady on her own terms, which do not flatter his ego.

Both the title and the first chapter of *The Egoist* underline the paradigmatic nature of the story. As his name implies, Sir Willoughby Patterne is a type rather than an individual; throughout the novel he performs with entire consistency, and his history can be summed up epigrammatically: "Through very love of self himself he slew."[16] The first chapter, repeating ideas from the *Essay,* ties together Meredith's theory of the social value of comedy and the application of this theory to the novel it introduces. Comedy, Meredith maintains here, is the "inward mirror" condensing common wisdom into easily "digestible" portions. Sir Willoughby's story is one of these portions, more diverting and instructive than a scientific case study ("We have little to learn of apes, and they may be left" [3]). As elsewhere in his works Meredith looks somewhat skeptically at the claims of science to improve man's self-knowledge, and he blames the literalness of naturalism—the plodding transcription of biological as well as emotional life—for the "modern malady of sameness." Comedy, on the other hand, cuts through the welter of facts by focusing on their social significance, thus clarifying our vision and providing a shortcut to wisdom.

Both in contents and in its paradoxical expression the summarizing epigram cited above suggests a dead end for Willoughby's story. It symbolizes an entrapment of egoism in the relentless dynamics of its own rationale, which the novel follows and contrasts with the liberating forces of genuine love.

On a walk in Patterne Park, when her companion Laetitia Dale asks whether she enjoys the park, Clara gives vent to her frustrations: "I chafe at restraints. Hedges and palings everywhere! I should have to travel ten years to sit down contented among these fortifications" (1:183). Clara, of course, feels hemmed in less by the restraints of the estate than by the banality of the owner. The structure of *The Egoist* is as Willoughby-centered as the setting; we understand Clara's claustrophobic reaction. One of Willoughby's ambitions is to keep his friends chained to a patriarchal paradise of his own making; the novel, however, shows a hell founded precisely on the enchaining of human affection and imagination, and affecting not the outcasts of his circle but those within, most obviously Sir Willoughby himself. Willoughby's amazement and fury at Clara's resistance to an Edenic captivity reveal deeper and deeper recesses of an inner hell in himself.

The danger in such a narrative method is that the reader, rather than being refreshed by comic laughter, experiences a claustrophobic reaction of his own. The relentlessness of comedy becomes oppressive when it demolishes Willoughby as effectively as a surrender to his "paradise" would demolish Clara. Meredith comes close to destroying the corrective function of comedy by overworking its severity. Only by also focusing on Clara and tracing *her* growth from egoistical self-enchainment to the psychological freedom she reaches at the end can he reaffirm the social value of the "game" of comedy. While we watch Willoughby pursued by the comic imps, our reaction is a mixture of horror and pity—horror because of his persisting moral stupidity, pity because we come to see him as pathetic, as much a victim of his author as of himself. Moreover, like Robert Louis Stevenson, who feared Meredith had used him as a model for Willoughby, the reader recognizes too many common human traits in the protagonist to feel comfortably detached. If this figure represents "all of us," as Meredith said, the outlook for civilization seems grim indeed.[17]

Willoughby is a handsome, cultivated, eminently eligible gentleman, adored from childhood on and now the "sun" of the county. But he is also a "prince": having been brought up to be adored, he must always be adorable. In fact, as the exposure of Willoughby in the novel makes clear, to be adored and adorable constitutes the

mainspring of his being. He has no genuine talents or aspirations—
he merely dabbles in science and politics—but he has built up an ide-
alized self out of the popular adulation his position has given him.
That he is a nonentity and a puppet, dependent on the world he pre-
tends to disdain, never becomes quite clear to him; the novel, however, insists on it, from the ironic encomium of the "leg" in chapter
2 to Willoughby's groveling pursuit of Laetitia in chapter 49.

How hollow Willoughby is becomes apparent in the "love-season
. . . the carnival of egoism" (1:130). As an able "hunter," he is
proud to have overcome his competition and won Clara, whose charm
will compliment his taste and whose unsullied purity, apart from en-
hancing her social value, will ensure an uncritical veneration of him.
Clara is to be the chief adorer in his circle; she is to prop up his self-
esteem in the face of the "world" and his nagging self-doubts. With
Clara as an increasingly restless listener, he "explains" himself to her
in fervent monologues designed to tie her irretrievably to himself as
well as to reassure himself about his general excellence. But the
monologues have the opposite effect: they disenchant her ("He slew
imagination" [2:183]) and make her long for the world.

When Clara resists his efforts to absorb her, a different Willoughby
emerges. For it is not quite true that he is a nonentity: he harbors
pride of Satanic proportions. In addition, through a shift in metaphor
from the images of his glory (sun, prince, king) to those of feeding,
devouring, hunting, and tormenting, Meredith reveals an underlying
core of brutality inconsistent with his gentlemanly appearance but
only too common, Meredith asserts, among upper-class males. Under
the veneer of the prince lurks the savage whose evolution into genuine
civilization has been prevented by a too indulgent upbringing. When
Willoughby's egoism is denied adulation, he turns to revenge. He envisions Clara's repentant return in melodramatic scenes taken from
popular fiction (chapter 23) and charged with eroticism. Later, induced by jealousy, he imagines marriage with a resisting bride: "It
would be a good roasting fire for her too, should she be averse. To
conceive her aversion was to burn her and devour her. She would then
be his! What say you? Burnt and devoured" (1:276). As he pursues
her, always restrained by the rules of polite manners and his self-
image, which cannot admit this savagery to himself, his fears and
frustrations "burn and devour" himself. They lead him to the practical
mistake of proposing to Laetitia, by which he gives up his trump card
of constancy, and to desperate maneuvers, designed to blind the

world to his second jilting. Though the world is not entirely taken in, it connives in protecting his pride: "The policy of the county is to keep him in love with himself," says the county's most perceptive lady, Mrs. Mountstuart. "When his pride is at ease he is a prince" (2:331). Comedy spares him at least social exposure.

Meredith shows distinct hostility to his protagonist. Whatever Willoughby says or does is either, in itself, absurd or subject to ironic authorial comment on his underlying motives. Significantly, the metaphors used by him and about him resemble those employed by the husband in "Modern Love," an earlier egoist jilted by a woman. There can be little doubt that in *The Egoist*, as in the poem, Meredith is still punishing himself for his vindictiveness toward Mary Nicolls, his first wife.

Meredith's portrayal of Clara is—perhaps for this reason—deeply understanding and sympathetic. She is the first in a series of heroines who allow Meredith to dramatize the inadequacy of Victorian attitudes toward sex and marriage. He especially ridicules the conventional requirement of complete sexual ignorance in a young woman. Clara's choice of Willoughby, abetted and strenuously upheld by her father, whose disdain for female emotions equals his love for Willoughby's old port, is excused by her inexperience and social pressure. Her visit to Patterne Hall opens her eyes not only to Willoughby's egoism but also to the implications of marital life. Her psychological resistance to her fiancé's oppressive "tenderness" expresses itself in an unmistakable sexual frigidity, which Willoughby prizes as modesty. Her combined emotional and physical aversion reveals itself in little gestures and incidents: "The gulf of a caress hove in view like an enormous billow hollowing under the curled ridge. She stooped to a buttercup; the monster swept by" (1:153).

Apparently helplessly bound by the engagement, Clara blames fate for her inability to extricate herself. She is tempted to do her duty and marry Willoughby despite her aversion. According to Meredith's moral system, this is *her* egoism—a reliance on conventions and fate. But she is not just a figure of porcelain; she has a vigorous mind and a sense of humor which enable her to overcome the egoistical lassitude threatening to overwhelm her. She learns, first of all, that loving is more necessary to her than being loved. Then, under Vernon's guidance, she learns to confront her problem rather than run away from it, to be patient, and to play fair. Returning to Willoughby rather than fleeing is a risky act for her, and she can do it only with her conscious will held momentarily in abeyance by physical exhaustion. But the next few days give her time to know herself better, to win important allies, and to gain her release through Willoughby's own fatuity. And since she succeeds in all this without causing a scandal, she becomes an adult socially as well as sexually and emotionally.

The Egoist contains only two other major characters, Vernon Whitford and Laetitia Dale. Laetitia, the sunflower to Willoughby's sun, much admired by the county for the constancy of her love, is a counterpart in egoism to Willoughby. Her flaw lies in her sentimental and purposeless self-sacrifice; she finds a pleasure in unrequited love. When Willoughby returns from a journey and, upon greeting her, finds himself reflected in her adoring eyes (1:29–30), the incident is a comment on her sentimentality as well as on his narcissism. Laetitia grows through her friendship with Clara, which opens her eyes to the true nature of her idol. At the end, when she proclaims herself an egoist, she has cast off her self-indulgent suffering for an unromantic pragmatism that may be less pleasant but more healthy for Willoughby.

Contrasted with Willoughby the sun king is Vernon, "Phoebus Apollo turned fasting friar," according to the aphoristic Mrs. Mountstuart (1:11). The metaphor stresses his reasonableness and self-control; he is one of Meredith's socially advanced thinkers and true friends of women. He is also associated with images suggesting freedom and expansion. Clara sees him sleeping under a blooming wild cherry tree:

She turned her face to where the load of virginal blossom, whiter than summer cloud on the sky, showered and drooped and clustered so thick as to claim colour and seem, like higher Alpine snows in noon-sunlight, a flush of white. From deep to deeper heaven of white, her eyes perched and soared. . . . Her reflection was: "He must be good who loves to lie and sleep beneath the branches of this tree!" (1:134–35)

The cherry tree, a potent symbol of hope in Meredith's works, suggests the openness, beauty, and variety of an Alpine landscape. Vernon shares Clara's love for the Alps, and both of them imagine personal growth and the growth of their love in terms of mountain climbing. Instead of the narrowness and flatness of Willoughby's company, Vernon offers a life of challenge and imaginative freedom.

In the structure of the novel Vernon has an important additional function: he prevents the "palpable climaxes" a reader would expect in comedy. He persuades Clara to return to Patterne Hall rather than flee. Later, although he knows of Willoughby's breach of faith, he does not force a dramatic exposure but waits for him to come to terms with Clara. Not that he protects him from the consequences of egoism: with his sparkle of suppressed laughter, he is too much the Comic Spirit for that. But by ensuring that the climaxes take place *within* the individual's soul, where they may lead to some insight, he observes the rules of comedy, which demand perfect civility. If comedy is a game played in the drawing room of civilized men and women, Vernon Whitford is a superb player—better, in fact, than his author, whose pursuit of the protagonist comes close to overstepping the rules of the game.

The Tragic Comedians

The Tragic Comedians (1880; serialized October 1880–February 1881 in the *Fortnightly Review*) takes its plot from a historical source and follows it so closely that the names of even secondary characters can easily be traced to their originals.[18] The historical source was the memoirs of Princess Racowitza, a German noblewoman. In the 1860s, the princess had loved the Hungarian-Jewish socialist Ferdinand Lassalle, who was an important figure in German politics but completely unacceptable to the young woman's family. In a duel with one of her other suitors, whom she subsequently married, he was fatally injured. Meredith found her memoirs shallow and self-serving and conveyed this impression into his novel; his heroine, Clothilde von Rüdiger, is complacent, weak, and, at best, pathetic—much like Sir Willoughby—whereas the hero, Sigismund Alvan, had the author's obvious sympathy.

In many ways the novel is a counterpart of *The Egoist:* the same situation—a man jilted—is subjected to comic scrutiny. But in Alvan the comic is subordinated to a more generous analysis, which, although clearly noting his flaws, also indicates his potential greatness. In fact, in view of his suffering and the apparent inevitability of the destruction of the couple's love, it becomes difficult to speak about comedy at all. Since the outcome of the story was given and commonly known, Meredith could demonstrate here from actuality what he had only imaginatively suggested in *The Egoist:* the force of man's passions underlying and always threatening the thin layer of his civilization.

Clothilde, an ambitious and quick-witted coquette, and Alvan are attracted to each other because of their apparent similarity in thought and speech. Although this similarity is only superficial, they fall in love. Clothilde's fear of her parents keeps the relationship dormant, while she encourages the devotion of another suitor, Prince Marko. But when the two lovers meet again in Switzerland, Alvan decides, with her approval, to ask her parents formally for her hand. Frightened by her family's anger, Clothilde flees to Alvan, ready to elope; he, however, insists on correct procedure and sends her back, confident both of his persuasiveness and the strength of her love. He is mistaken in both. The family resists, and she is too weak to withstand the alternate torments and pleadings to which she is subjected. She comes to doubt Alvan's love; when his emissaries interview her, she conveys to them an impression of cold indifference, although she hopes they will recognize her continuing loyalty to Alvan. When she refuses a personal interview with him—still hoping, however, for his help—Alvan, after months of futile efforts, vents his frustration in a furious letter and challenges her father to a duel. Prince Marko accepts the challenge for her father and kills Alvan. Emotionally exhausted, Clothilde accepts Marko as her husband.

With its linked motifs of love at first sight and the adversity of fate, *The Tragic Comedians* calls to mind *Romeo and Juliet*. But Meredith makes clear that neither providence nor social discrepancy destroys their happiness. The tragedy results from their flaws: ambition, vanity, and blindness to their own limitations. Whereas Clothilde has little to show for her conceit except some superficial brightness, Alvan is a serious, far-thinking politician, and part of his tragedy—like Nevil Beauchamp's—is that he is deflected from his public task by petty personal considerations.

Alvan is "hugely man."[19] Physically and intellectually he is in the prime of life. He glories in his health, his personal magnetism, his political astuteness, his forward-looking mind. Like Willoughby, he tends toward self-defining speeches, perhaps hinting at an underlying sense of social inferiority, and like Willoughby, he has an ambiguous relationship with the "world." But in his enthusiasm for his work— particularly in his drive to educate and enfranchise the masses, of which Meredith clearly approves—and in his self-confidence, he is deeply appealing. Even his aggrandizing metaphors for himself speak more of a zest for life than of personal conceit.

"Barriers are for those who cannot fly" (34) is his motto. Clothilde believes she can fly over the barriers imposed by society; she sees herself as independent of mind. But for a husband she wants an "eagle" who will carry her aloft; the eagle must also be a gentleman. These images suggest her real lack of strength and her conventionality. Alvan soon realizes that she needs his support, but in his self-confidence he is convinced he can make her his equal. Clothilde is the Aurora to his sun; she is his child, his spring, his Paris, but also, more ominously, his gold-crested serpent, his golden sand, and his will o' the wisp. These images—and they are insistent throughout the novel, as Leonée Ormond has shown[20]—suggest the unstable and, indeed, treacherous nature of her love. A dead lichen-draped tree seen by both of them reappears later in Alvan's dream, the lichen turned to poisonous serpents associated with Clothilde.

Both characters overestimate themselves and each other. For all their ambition, they are bound to society and unable to "fly," and their independence of mind is somewhat theatrical. Clothilde half realizes this herself when she calls herself "three parts an actress" (85). Alvan shows a Philistine tendency in his choice of a well-born young lady and his insistence on the proper forms of courtship. Out of pride and ignorance of her, he rejects the "centaur and nymph" approach. But once he has given her back to the world, the story becomes a tangle of misreadings, doubts, recriminations, a self-indulgent fatalism on her part, and self-abasement and unethical plotting on his. It ends in brutal name-calling and the duel he would have disdained in a saner mood.

Meredith intersperses the scenes of Alvan's deterioration with others showing his rekindled hope, his longing for simple family life, his pathetic plans for his honeymoon, and his continuing desire to serve his fellowmen. The reader is drawn into the inner struggle of the "man of angels and devils." Alvan's final fury, however, is not shown directly; at his last appearance he is still hoping for a meeting with her: "So little a thing! His intellect weighed the littleness of it, but he had become level with it; he magnified it with the greatness of his desire" (176–77). Half interior speech, half authorial comment, the passage reveals the split between intellect and instinct. Shortly after, this split causes the hero to crash, like Phaeton, driver of the

sun wagon. As if to underscore the littleness of the person for whom
Alvan dies, Meredith coldly sums up Clothilde's self-pitying reaction:
"Her craven's instinct to make a sacrifice of others flew with claws of
hatred at her parents. . . . Providence and her parents were not forgiven. But as we are in her debt for some instruction, she may now
be suffered to go" (197, 201).

Although *The Tragic Comedians* is carefully constructed and relent-
lessly gripping, it is not one of Meredith's most successful novels.
Critics have called it overwrought and histrionic.[21] Meredith obviously thought that a character like Lassalle demanded a portrait com-
mensurate with his large ambitions, delusions, and suffering.
Dramatic concentration and a style rich in metaphor were suggested
by the historical facts. Thus the novel itself reflects the "fantastical"
material it is based on. But because Meredith's attitude toward Princess Racowitza was hostile from the start, he is blatantly unfair to
Clothilde. His contempt for her diminishes Alvan's judgment and
therefore the tragedy. It is only in *One of our Conquerors* (1891) that
Meredith creates a tragedy in which a woman, though weak, and a
man, though grandly deluded, fully and equally engage the reader's
sympathy. Alvan's overwrought history points directly to the "con-
queror" Victor Radnor; Clothilde, to Meredith's credit, has no succes-
sor in his fiction.

Diana of the Crossways

In *The Egoist* Meredith had dramatized the idea that comedy was
usually concerned with the battle of the sexes and that women, being
naturally more sensible than men, were closer to the Comic Spirit. In
Diana of the Crossways (1885; serialized June–December 1884 in the
Fortnightly Review) Meredith depicts in his heroine, Diana Merion, a
Clara Middleton without family protection, but with strong ambitions and a more complex mentality. It is the story of a spirited,
independent-minded young woman, whose native good sense makes her
an ally of comedy but whose reluctance to come to terms with herself
makes her vulnerable to the laughter of the Comic Spirit. Although
the novel has a conventional happy ending, its comedy is muted by
the occurrence of a severe illness, an attempted suicide, and the im-
minent death of the character who most obviously speaks for Meredith. In this novel Meredith affirms his goal of realism in fiction,
both through the story and through explicit authorial comment.

Diana Merion, a young Irish woman of exceptional beauty and wit, early experiences the unscrupulous attentions of male admirers. To avoid them, she marries an older man, Mr. Warwick. The marriage is a failure, and after she has formed a close but platonic friendship with an elder statesman, her jealous husband sues for divorce on grounds of infidelity. She is legally vindicated and no divorce takes place, but she resolves to live alone, supporting herself by writing novels. A young politician, Percy Dacier, wins her love, but her friend Emma Dunstane's serious illness prevents their elopement to the Continent and opens Diana's eyes to the folly of such an act. Although worried by financial difficulties and constantly subject to gossip, she helps Dacier in his career by giving small but brilliant parties for him. But she is distressed when he urges her to resume their former intimacy. In a state of panic, heightened by her financial worries, she betrays an important state secret he has told her. His fury at this act leads him to reject her instantly. Meanwhile, Mr. Warwick has died, and after a period of severe emotional illness and gradual recovery, with the help of Emma, Diana marries Thomas Redworth, who has long loved and supported her.

The action takes place about forty years before Meredith wrote the novel and is based on several scandalous incidents—true or rumored—surrounding the fascinating figure of Mrs. Caroline Norton, granddaughter of the Irish playwright Richard Sheridan.[22] Meredith made use of these incidents to show the precarious position of a woman who relies on her wits to live in advance of social norms, believing in the equality of the sexes and the possibility of true friendship between them. That he used a real model for his heroine was not unusual for him; many of his friends and acquaintances, and even his younger self, appear in his novels. It is unusual, however, to find Meredith appropriating so imaginatively a historical figure he did not know well. Mrs. Norton shared two attributes with him: she was "Celtic" and a novelist. Meredith wrote not only a novel about the "new woman," as Diana is often seen,[23] but also a study of the problems of the intellectual author and a vindication of his own fictional principles. Concentrating on one character, whose ethnic background is, for Meredith, synonymous with lively wit, but lacking in "Teutonic" solidity, Meredith draws what is even for him an uncommonly sensitive and sympathetic portrait.

In a notoriously difficult introduction Meredith explains the artistic principles on which *Diana* is based. By presenting the heroine first through entries in the diaries of her contemporaries, he suggests a historical rather than a fictional character. He does not intend, of course, to remind the reader that Diana was based on a historical person, but to emphasize his concern with psychological realism; Diana, he implies, has made a strong impression on her contemporaries because she is not the typical heroine of romance. (This type of female figure also appears in the novel in Dacier's eventual fiancée, Constance Asper.) Asserting that the literary taste of his own time would wrongly reject the reality of a mixed character in favor of either "rosy-pink" sentimentalism or "dirty-drab" naturalism, he pleads for an intelligent, realistic portrayal of human nature both in its outer actions and in its inner growth: "The brainstuff of fiction is internal history" (*Diana*, 17). The civilizing influence of realism—"philosophy in fiction"—is particularly necessary in drawing women, because Meredith sees the relationship between the sexes overshadowed by the "over-dainty" morality that contains its own "grossness." In Diana he presents a feminine image not appealing to puritan taste, a woman of disturbing unconventionality. He suggests, however, that an honest portrayal of her complex, growing nature can throw light not only on woman but on life itself.

Like Thomas Hardy in *Tess of the D'Urbervilles* a few years later, Meredith presents a "pure" woman—morally pure despite a host of male admirers and despite her husband's jealousy. She has no idea of playing on her sexual attractiveness. In fact, she is deeply disturbed when men whose friendship she has valued suddenly show ardent feelings. Her precipitate marriage to Warwick is explainable only by her wish for protection. After their separation she is delighted to live in a platonic world of intellectual work. Her impulsive agreement to elope with Dacier is based on her fear that her husband will force her back to his side. Her name, Diana, links her to the goddess of chastity and her strongest emotional bond is not with a man, but with her friend Emma.

Her sexual coldness, however, is only superficial, caused by her anger at the insignificant role of intelligent women in public life. Confronted with Dacier's passion, Diana is deeply distressed to discern that she too has strong sexual feelings. This discovery, along with anger at Dacier's boldness, blunts her normal intelligence so that she acts foolishly and irresponsibly. The reader has noted earlier instances of her submerged sexuality. For example, she enjoys recalling a summer vacation in the Italian Alps. Coming shortly after her separation from Warwick, it had seemed a recovery of her lost youth, but she gradually realizes that the charm of that time lies less in her remembered closeness to nature than in the fact that she first met Dacier then. Her "internal history" is the discovery of her sexual nature, a discovery she resists because it seems to deprive her of her proud self-sufficiency.

Ironically, Diana reveals her emotional life clearly enough in her novels, without being able to apply them to herself. Her fiction dramatizes the role she would like to play—Princess Egeria, chaste adviser-confidante—and the love she feels for Dacier, the "young Minister." Only at her crisis does she realize a similarity between her protagonist, "the Man of two Minds," and herself, "the woman likewise divided, if not similar" (358). Meredith wittily plays on this similarity between author and character, putting himself into the picture as well, for a synopsis of "The Man of Two Minds" suggests a likeness to his *Egoist,* and Diana's inability to go on with this work hints at Meredith's changed attitude toward pure comedy. Even more wittily, he first shows Diana dismissing the temptation of writing sensational fiction—although "her present mood was a craving for excitement; for incident, wild action, the primitive machinery of our species" (*Diana,* 360)—then follows with his own "wild action" of Dacier's passionate outburst and Diana's headlong drive to the editor to sell her secret. The reader is meant to see, of course, that these incidents are handled in a rather more sophisticated way than popular fiction would. The real excitement lies in the turbulent state of Diana's mind.

As she herself realizes early in the novel, Diana is a woman of several minds ("I'm at war with myself" [48]). On the one hand, she likes to be a social and intellectual success. On the other, she yearns for a pastoral existence, without the complications of sex, society, and money. A pastoral life would, of course, make novel writing impossible for her, since she depends on social figures for her subject matter. Living in society, however, has its obvious risks for an unattached woman unprovided for. Diana tries therefore to create for herself a pastoral existence in the midst of society. She fails ostensibly for financial reasons, but really because in her fierce self-sufficiency—masking the fear of her sexuality—she misjudges her own talents as well as the power of convention. Meredith does not slight the actual difficulties an unprotected woman of independent spirit faced in Victorian society or the pernicious effect the customary idealization of femininity had on women's minds. For all her wit and intelligence, Diana's mind is little developed or disciplined, as her thoughtless be-

trayal of the state secret shows. In fact, her wit gives her the false
idea that she can cope with reality by pressing it into aphorisms,
somewhat like Sir Austin in his "Pilgrim's Scrip," although with
more self-directed irony. In politics and the arts Diana is a dilettante,
although the realistic principles on which she bases her fiction—and
which Meredith overtly endorses—may lead her to better work if she
can free herself from the egocentricity of her vision.

Despite her sophistication, Diana is, for most of the novel, a
charming, precocious child with whom Meredith is enchanted. As
Gillian Beer has noted, the author's approach to her is split: on the
one hand, he draws her emotional crosscurrents with frankness and
sensitivity; on the other, he tries to protect her from the reader's verdict that she behaves foolishly.[24] He withholds the crucial scene of her
betrayal, blackens Dacier's character arbitrarily, and inserts frequent
authorial comments exonerating her. When he tells us, "Poor Diana
was the flecked heroine of Reality: not always the same; not impecca-
ble; not an ignorant-innocent, nor a guileless: good under good leading . . . a growing soul" (399), he loads the dice for his heroine.
When he calls her a "princess of her kind and time, but a foreign
one . . . and has no dolly-dolly compliance" (*Diana,* 441), he actually
imitates Diana's egoistical attitude, setting her apart from the rest of
society and simultaneously betraying his own disdain for the world of
common fiction readers.

It is not the narrator-commentator who represents the best of Meredith in this novel, but one of his characters. Emma Dunstane, whose
love for Diana is obvious, but whose mental discipline and reasonableness enable her to see her friend's faults and needs, responds to the
brittleness and emotional shallowness of Diana's wit with silence. Yet
she is instrumental in bringing about the marriage of Diana and the
solid Englishman Thomas Redworth, for she realizes, in the face of
death, that what is necessary in human life is not the proud isolation
of the intelligent character, but personal and social integration. The
union of the Celt and the Saxon, the artistic and the practical temperament, represents an embrace of contrasts promising well for future
generations. Meredith's own "embrace of contrasts"—the fusion of
poetry and analysis in a realistic novel—is less successful, not quite
steering clear of the "rosy-pink" of sentimentalism in the depiction of
his heroine. But like Diana herself, this novel points forward to future achievements, in two of Meredith's last three novels.

Chapter Five

The Last Novels: "An Index for the Enlargement of Your Charity"

Like the last novels by Henry James, and for somewhat similar reasons, Meredith's fiction of the 1890s makes large demands on the reader's patience and acuity. In the three completed novels—*One of Our Conquerors* (1891), *Lord Ormont and His Aminta* (1894), and *The Amazing Marriage* (1895)—the writer's handling of plot and language often seems recklessly and arbitrarily self-indulgent. As the contemporary reviews of these books testify, he comes close to severing the bond between author and audience, even for an "acute minority" (*Belloni*, 2:230), because he appears to care little for economy and clarity in structure; and his style, veering between the highly Latinate mock-heroic and the poetically condensed, betrays a radical distrust of common prose. He carries his concern with "internal history" (*Diana*, 17) to the point where the telling of it is fraught with epistemological and semantic problems, and then backs off in his final novel to conclude an uneasy truce between analysis and the common human impulse to simply gossip, tell stories, and exclaim over them in plain language.

Meredith disingenuously complained to Clement Shorter in 1891, when *One of Our Conquerors* had just been published: "It seems, from the general attack on the first sentence of my last novel, that literary playfulness in description is antipathetic to our present taste" (*Letters*, 2:1029). Literary playfulness is really not the issue here. In his last novels Meredith explores the ability of language to distort as well as convey reality. He is concerned with the danger of self-deception through rhetoric—a concern already evident in *Diana of the Crossways*, but now including public as well as private speech. Like many of his progressive friends, Meredith saw in the debates of the 1880s much evidence of muddled thinking and a general refusal to come to terms with changing social conditions, despite a veneer of pseudoliberalism.

Owing to an agricultural depression and widespread unemployment, England's social and political situation in the 1880s was alarming; but instead of taking care of England's domestic problems, including the vexing Irish question, the political leaders directed the people's dreams and ambitions toward a romantically varnished imperialism that would lead to international complications, particularly with Germany. Meredith was disturbed by the chauvinistic and materialistic attitude of most public voices, which manifested itself in a cliché-riddled, jingoistic style. In his late novels he attempts to expose the shallowness of contemporary political thought by bringing dead words and phrases back to life, by the sheer accumulation of hackneyed expressions and circumlocutions, and by a syntax that at times sounds German or Latin rather than English.[1]

At its best, Meredith's verbal agility leads to a richly suggestive textual fabric, alerting the reader to unspoken meanings and pervasive splits between acts and underlying emotions. At its worst, Meredith's play with language excludes us from the imaginative cooperation among author, reader, and content that is the basis of all fiction. This happens most often when Meredith explores the border area between unarticulated feelings and their transformation into articulated thought, as he does intensely in his last novels. Here language can work only by suggestion through analogy and symbol—"all the fraternity of old lamps for lighting our abysmal darkness" (*OOC*, 314). But overcomplexity of figurative language has its danger; instead of helping the reader to "vault over gaps and thickets and dreary places" (*OOC*, 189), the text calls undue attention to itself. When we are asked to share a character's unarticulated emotions, especially if complex and unstable, a proliferation of metaphors is apt to distract. Significantly, Meredith's most mature characters—for example, Vernon Whitford in *The Egoist*—are alert to the problems inherent in figurative speech. And as D. S. Austin has shown, Meredith's own uneasiness about the value of metaphor runs through his entire work in numerous ambivalent comments.[2]

Intimately linked with his distrust of contemporary rhetoric, Meredith's social criticism in the 1890s is more extensive than ever. In *One of Our Conquerors* he satirizes the hypocritical gestures of a society committed to a preservation of the status quo. In *Lord Ormont,* much less rigorously or successfully, he castigates British complacency in military and intellectual matters. In *The Amazing Marriage* he exposes the purposelessness and spiritual vacuity of the upper class. Most important, all three novels show a deep awareness of the way communal disorders are related to the roles society assigns to women. Specifically, Meredith's studies of the institution of marriage as a private and public phenomenon link social and psychological analysis. He demonstrates that in a conventional marriage, the proprietary nature of which reflects the possessiveness of traditional society, women are not allowed to work effectively for the good of communal life but are, instead, forced to employ devious and potentially destructive methods to assert themselves. In the marriage of equal partners, which Meredith projects in vague outline in each of the three novels, society as a whole benefits from women's innate common sense, strength of feeling, and capacity for sympathy.

From *The Egoist* on, Meredith had advanced an overtly feminist position, drawing increasingly radical conclusions about women's rights and institutionalized sexual relationships.[3] In Clara Middleton and Diana Warwick he had drawn young women who dared to oppose the norm, at least temporarily, but who did not actually break marriage vows. In *One of Our Conquerors* a marriage vow has been broken; Meredith condemns the marriage, which had been purely mercenary, and upholds the adultery. Yet he censures the flaunting of the illicit relationship upon which the plot turns, because like the previous marriage it serves mercenary ends: the male protagonist uses it and his partner to consolidate his social status. In a subplot involving the rescue of a fallen woman, Meredith pleads overtly for an enlargement of social charity and an end to the double standard that condones promiscuity in the male while condemning the woman. In *Lord Ormont* he presents the paradoxical situation of a legitimate but unacknowledged marriage and allows the woman, who suffers from this ambiguous position, to break her bond for an adulterous but personally satisfying one. The blurred and inconclusive analysis of motives makes this novel an artistic failure, although its emancipated view of marriage comes across with startling bluntness. Finally, in *The Amazing Marriage,* Meredith tests the social and psychological impact of a marriage on its partners, this time choosing the opposite of the situation in *Lord Ormont*—a socially acknowledged bond but a rejection of all personal obligations by the husband, who deserts his wife immediately after the wedding. The novel suggests that a marriage even as defective as this one has its own vitality; both partners mature to some

extent. But *The Amazing Marriage* also indicates the limits of resilience in this relationship and sets competing bonds, ultimately more
powerful, alongside it.

In the three novels the male partners are guilty of regarding their
wives as possessions to be flaunted, used, and neglected at will. Significantly, these men are also—despite their prominent social positions—isolated from their fellowmen and incapable of genuine male
friendships. They seek others only for transitory gratification of their
vanity or other egoistical purposes. In contrast, friendships between
women flourish, effectively encouraging and supporting the growth of
independent-minded, fair, and loyal personalities. Although Meredith shows the collective "British matron" ruling over the communal
morals as severely as ever, his heroines are marked by a generosity of
spirit that recognizes the potentialities of good in their weaker sisters
and inspires them to look beyond their degrading circumstances.

This generosity, Meredith suggests, could redeem society as a
whole. If allowed to flourish, it would inspire men to social justice as
well as to superb cultural and intellectual feats. It could, in fact, lead
civilization out of the stagnation and decay in which Meredith saw it
trapped. The unsatisfactory marriages his last three novels portray are
emblematic of what he found wrong with society. But Meredith also
envisions the possibility of social wholeness: individually, in a marriage of partners who will not exploit each other, and collectively, in
a society where women can actively assert themselves and where charity frees both men and women from the debilitating results of sexual
warfare.

One of Our Conquerors

For many students of Victorian fiction, *One of Our Conquerors* (1891;
serialized in the *Fortnightly Review* October 1890–May 1891) is a major challenge to their appreciation of Meredith's art. From its first appearance it was greeted with consternation, dismay, and, at times,
derision. The *Times* acknowledged the excellence of its ideas but was
disturbed by its style, as have been many other readers, past and present: "Could Mr. Meredith's ideas but be reduced into lucid English!
But his is one of those cases in which form and matter seem inseparable. He is, apparently, incapable of sending the most profound truth
or the most obvious truism into the world until he has worked it up
laboriously into epigram or anagram."[4] The *Saturday Review* was more

hostile: "The author's usual faults of incoherence, prolixity, strain-ing after epigram, seeking after the uncommon, lack of firmness in character-drawing, and allusiveness, are intensified in his latest work. . . . He has a story, . . . but it will not let itself be told."[5] After a scathing review in the *Spectator*, J. A. Noble concluded, "To describe *One of Our Conquerors* as a good novel is impossible."[6]

While admitting the verbal and structural difficulties of the novel, a modern critic, schooled in the complexities of Joyce, Faulkner, and later writers, can see in *One of Our Conquerors* a genuine if flawed artis-tic achievement. Despite its digressions, evasions, and paradoxes—or perhaps because of them since its form and matter are indeed insepa-rable—the novel rewards the careful reader with a disturbing and moving experience. Far from being a literary performance lacking es-sential vitality, as Siegfried Sassoon asserted, *One of Our Conquerors* contains, embedded in the very extravagance of its style and struc-ture, a lively picture and an urgent critique of late-Victorian society extraordinary in both breadth and depth of conception.[7]

One of Our Conquerors is the story of Victor Radnor, an attractive, cultivated, highly successful business tycoon in late nineteenth-cen-tury London. As the title suggests, he is the hero of his age and the representative of its ambitions and achievements. His roles as family man, friend, patron of the arts, philanthropist, and parliamentary candidate allow Meredith to examine contemporary social life from various aspects; moreover, Victor's private and public history are es-sentially one, and this identity and its denial by Victor himself form the basis for the novel.

The ambiguity of the title—"our" may also suggest "one who con-quers us"—calls attention to Meredith's preoccupation with the shifty and unreliable nature of language and its perversion by ideology, one of the central themes in the novel.[8] Victor's fate, England's fate, and the complexities of verbal communication are made to appear closely related. The novel questions how far language can distort truth; Vic-tor, like England, attempts to negate his past through words and is in turn destroyed by his inability to distinguish, in the present, be-tween facts and words.

The main action spans one year. Victor has built a new country seat for his family, but since Nataly, his wife, finds it too ostentatious, his pride in it is spoilt, and they never live there. Their daughter, Nesta, befriends a "fast" woman and persuades the lady's lover to marry her. Nesta herself is courted by a circumspect and conventional young lord

who dislikes Nesta's progressive ideas. She eventually engages herself
to Dartrey Fenellan, a family friend who shares her sympathy for
fallen women. Victor and Nataly drift emotionally apart. They pay a
visit to a dying old woman with whom they lived twenty years ago;
soon after, while Victor is campaigning for a parliamentary seat, first
Nataly and then the old woman die on the same day. Victor goes in-
sane and dies from grief a year later.

The simplicity of the story is deceptive, for the present lives of
Victor and Nataly are shadowed by the past of twenty years ago. We
see this part intrude continually, as we learn that Victor and Nataly
have never married; that Victor is the husband of the old woman,
from whom he eloped with Nataly and who refuses to give him a divorce; that Victor and Nataly's daughter does not know of their legal
irregularity; and that "Mrs. Burman," Victor's legal wife, has apparently sown enough rumors that complete social acceptance has so far
eluded him and Nataly. Victor may be a financial and political con-
queror; he has yet to conquer Mrs. Burman, and this he tries to do
in the course of the novel.

One of Our Conquerors exploits the irony that in his very anticipation
of triumph, Victor is conquered because he has mistaken his enemy.
Although Mrs. Burman shadows his life, what causes his tragedy is
not his past trespass—the elopement with Nataly—but the way he
has thought and lived ever since. Because there is a mystery about
Mrs. Burman in the novel—she is a persistent object of rumors and
Victor's speculations but does not appear in person until quite late—
the reader is tempted to share Victor's belief that she is a decisive part
of his life: an embodiment of fate, the favorite excuse of Meredith's
sentimentalists. Yet the novel demonstrates through Victor's uninten-
tional but inexorable destruction of his bond with Nataly that he
alone is responsible for his fall. Because he has been unable to learn
from his past—he has, in fact, never renounced his purely mercenary
motives in marrying Mrs. Burman in the first place—his early egoism
has been exacerbated, and Nataly becomes his second victim.

Victor exhibits the self-destructive egoism Meredith exposes
throughout his fiction. But because he is portrayed as the quintessence of the contemporary Briton, his history also reflects Meredith's
conviction that England, refusing to come to terms with its legacy of
social injustice, is on a suicidal course. This theme, anticipated in
Harry Richmond twenty years earlier, receives an added urgency from

Meredith's fear that rhetorical language can actually increase the danger. The glibly articulate and witty society conceals from itself, under a veneer of garrulousness, the fact that its members no longer truly communicate.

Victor's first appearance is emblematic of his history and the breakdown of social relations. After he has slipped on a banana peel and fallen down on London Bridge, he is helped up by a workman, whose hands leave stains on Victor's white vest. Upon Victor's genial complaint, the workman rebuffs him with "And none of your damn punctilio" (3), a response that—along with the fall itself—upsets Victor because he feels himself unjustly attacked. For several chapters Meredith transcribes, by stream-of-consciousness technique, Victor's attempts to regain his composure; Victor's enterprises in the later chapters are extensions of this aim. Victor is incessantly protecting and defending himself—against Mrs. Burman, against recollection of the unpleasant encounter with the workman, against his uneasy awareness of social tensions in his country.

On the surface Victor appears as an unwavering optimist. Conditioned by his financial successes, he tells himself that he was born for happiness and that the "clearsighted celestial Powers" (*OOC,* 13) have long forgiven the trespass of his elopement with Nataly. And the report of Mrs. Burman's final readiness for divorce, along with rumors of a terminal illness, seems to confirm his self-appraisal. His friends are so conditioned by his invincible optimism and his actual successes that they adopt his version of reality, thus adding to his conviction that "all is coming right—must come right" (*OOC,* 44).

But Victor's optimism is a whistling in the dark. Like all of Meredith's protagonists, he is a divided man. Interior monologues betray his fear of being finally *not* correct in his version of reality. He is a solipsist who suspects his solipsism and who therefore craves the opposition of his friends but only to defeat it, and with it, again and again, his self-doubt.[9] Paradoxically, it would be lifesaving for him to be proved fundamentally wrong; but his mind, fatally constituted for happiness, cheerfully absorbs, trivializes, and disarms all opposition. He dislikes satire. Instead, he is addicted to thinking in metaphors and similes, which rob experience of its immediate impact, playing up the liveliness of his imagination and his verbal virtuosity. From the beginning this virtuosity is at work on self-deception; by exaggerating the importance of a trifling incident—the slip on the banana peel—Victor trivializes the real importance of his other fall, the loss of social feeling demonstrated in his encounter with the workman and recurring throughout in his flawed relationship with Nataly.

The most obvious sign of the flaw in this union is Victor's and Nataly's contrasting attitudes toward Lakelands. For Victor, this splendid country seat is to be the ultimate triumph over his past and an affirmation of social respectability; for Nataly, it means a flaunting of their irregular relationship in defiance of conventions she innately respects. Lakelands becomes for her, by anticipation, an instrument of punishment. Other facts equally point to the breakdown of their marriage. Their daughter, Nesta, for example, brings out both the strength and the limitation of their love. Her innate common sense and charity and her choice of Dartrey Fenellan, one of Meredith's ideal masculine figures, prove "that the father and mother had kept faith with Nature" (OOC, 514). Yet she also illumines her parents' faults. For her father she is a plaything and, like Lakelands, a pawn in his scheme for social triumph. By contrast, Nataly sees in Nesta's coming of age a threat of social exposure and the necessity to confront and articulate the facts she tries to hide even from herself—notably, her growing disillusionment with Victor.[10] Most alarmingly, she finds in Nesta's independence of moral judgment a threatening evidence of the same moral laxness of which she accuses herself.

Toward the end of the novel, in the crucial scene of their visit to Mrs. Burman, the couple are directly confronted with their past. Ironically, the mysterious Mrs. Burman is only a tired woman facing death and therefore willing to forgive. She becomes the third test for their relationship. For Nataly, the visit is an expiation, releasing her from her mute isolation into a deeper understanding of Nesta. In contrast, Victor manages to "conquer" even the confrontation with his past; that is, he makes a performance of it. During his visit, he counts the minutes, reflects sentimentally on the passage of time, makes small talk, kneels to pray, and "after a repetition of his short form of prayer deeply stressed, he thanked himself with the word 'sincere,' and a queer side-thought on our human susceptibility to the influence of posture. We are such creatures" (OCC, 489). Victor feels himself to be as released from the past as Nataly really is, but unlike her, he is now more eager than ever to pursue the conquest of the world: "Now that Mrs. Burman, on her way to bliss, was no longer the dungeon-cell for the man he would show himself to be, this name for successes, . . . this Victor Montgomery Radnor, intended impressing himself upon the world as a factory of ideas" (493).

It is characteristic of Nataly's development and Victor's lack of it that Lakelands, Nesta, and Mrs. Burman change in significance for Nataly, whereas they stay the same for Victor. The facts that Lakelands becomes a torment, that Nesta changes from embodied guilt to a promise for the future, and that Mrs. Burman changes from social threat to fellow sufferer point to Nataly's capacity for growth. Her illness, symbol of her conscience and made fatal by her habitual self-repression, becomes paradoxically redemptive, not because it is a superstitious payment for a past sin, but because suffering makes her sympathetic to the suffering of others.[11] For Victor, Nataly's changes are incomprehensible, though he manages to trivialize them in his usual condescending playfulness. Victor himself stays the same throughout the novel; his final madness has been foreshadowed from the beginning and develops organically—a disregard of reality so complete that it becomes irrevocable.

Throughout the novel Meredith tempts the reader to share Victor's delusions. The idyll of Victor's family life, with its music, friends, and travels, and the sterling qualities of his daughter seem to confirm his view of himself. The effect of his friend Colney Durance's pessimism, which could counteract his complacency, is weakened by excess; Nataly's moral timidity has a self-indulgence of its own, redeemed only late in the novel by her suffering and by her one act of courage—telling Nesta's fiancé of her illegitimacy. Mrs. Burman long appears malevolent and mysteriously powerful. At the end, the reader is tempted to ascribe Nataly's death to the "celestial Powers" as just punishment for her and Victor's early transgression. But although the exact time of her death is a capricious stroke of fate, it has little causal connection with their guilt.[12] Here Meredith challenges the reader to distinguish the morally relevant consequences of an act from those that merely seem so. Indeed, in a more general sense as well, the key to the novel lies in this challenge to distinguish and choose what is relevant to a coherent vision of life from a welter of seemingly unrelated details.

Imaging the incoherence of Victor's thinking, the structure of *One of Our Conquerors* abounds in symptoms of incoherence, particularly in the frequent apparently irrelevant plot digressions. Undoubtedly some of them, such as the family's excursion to France, have little structural significance. Others—for example, chapter 23, the narration of a dog's misbehavior and its mistresses' consequent loss of sleep—advance the action in an irritatingly ponderous and pretentious manner. But this ridiculous episode, further slowed by mock-epic authorial digressions, makes a genuine point: it satirizes the overdaintiness of Victorian society, its genteel reluctance to deal with anything unsavory, whether a dog's mess or a niece's doubtful background; and the implicit fussy equation of the two issues comments on contemporary moral standards. [13]

The mock-epic voice is evident from the start of the novel in a notorious sentence of over eighty words that invests an archetypal comic scene (a man's slip on a banana peel) with an ironic dignity. [14] But as the reader is drawn into the stream-of-consciousness passages following this incident, he realizes that Victor himself uses mock-heroic language, partly to make fun of himself—for he is quite able to do that and thus disarm any potential self-reproaches—and partly to keep his mind disengaged from the claims of the world upon him. For the reader the demarcation between the protagonist projecting his genial, sometimes rueful view of life and the narrator defining a larger reality is blurred; he has to penetrate a text that may be the play of Victor's mind as much as the analysis of this mind by the narrator.

As we become more sensitive to Victor's shortcomings, we also grow suspicious of the garrulous narrator—all the more so since Nataly's speechless suffering and Nesta's quiet factualness are conveyed by a different voice, both terser and more poetic. Victor's voluble self-defensive optimism, echoed by his friends and by the general tone of the novel, is qualified by the actual happenings past and present, which the reader must judge for himself. In this act of discovering the true story, we see the innumerable incidental comments on contemporary issues, which crowd the novel and in which earlier critics have found instances of Meredith's lack of discipline, take on a new function. One of Our Conquerors remarks on countless social, cultural, and political topics through Victor and his friends or through the narrator. The comments are often shrewd and reflect many of Meredith's favorite ideas; some go to the heart of the novel. [15] But in the context of the story, the necessity for England to guard itself against foreign competition, the virtues of boxing or the Salvation Army, the qualities of the Welsh, and the superiority of German over Italian opera are less important than they appear. What is important is the reader's impression of a general competence: the narrator, Victor, and his circle all seem thoughtful, at home in the world, aware of its shortcomings, yet managing gracefully and even wittily. As the plot develops, this competence becomes questionable, then hollow, and finally, in Victor's mad babbling, a travesty of itself. It reveals itself as a mass of incessant and incoherent attempts to control the course of public life while foiling self-scrutiny. And this, Meredith implies, is the state of affairs in contemporary England.

Incoherence is the subject of Meredith's novel, in Victor's private history and in the society of which he is epitome and hero. Incoherence—a manic accumulation of metaphors, minor characters, and episodic digressions—marks its structure. Yet the ultimate effect of *One of Our Conquerors* is one of coherence, for Victor's movement toward madness has a convincing logic. Once we recognize Mrs. Burman for what she is and, unlike Victor, dismiss her for the more pertinent comment on life offered by Nataly and Nesta, the pieces fall into place. Nataly's suffering and death and Nesta's courageous vision of the future contain and contradict the histrionics of the self-deceiver, giving the novel a poignancy and depth of vision easily overlooked in the reader's first struggle with the difficult text, but amply rewarding repeated readings.

Lord Ormont and His Aminta

Meredith's next novel, *Lord Ormont and His Aminta* (1894; serialized in *Pall Mall Magazine,* December 1893–August 1894), signaled a decline in his creative energy and intellectual control. Ironically, the reviewers were generally kind to it; the *Literary World,* in Boston, even proclaimed it as ranking "among his very best novels; perhaps it is destined to be the most popular of all."[16] Negative reviews repeated their strictures against Meredith's style; others predictably complained about the treatment of the moral question—Aminta's desertion of her husband for a younger man. An exceptionally unfavorable reaction came from Henry James. In a letter to Edmund Gosse on 22 August 1894, he commented on the "unspeakable *Lord Ormont*":

It fills me with a critical rage, an artistic fury, utterly blighting in me the indispensable principle of respect. . . . All elaborate predicates of exposition without the ghost of a nominative to hook themselves to; and not a difficulty met, not a figure presented, not a scene constituted—not a dim shadow condensing once either into audible or into visible reality.[17]

James lashes out at the evasions and ellipses particularly prominent in this novel. More recent critics have tended to agree with his poor opinion of it, pointing not only to its artistic flaws but also to the emotional self-indulgence evident in it.[18] *Lord Ormont* raises but then blinks a number of issues; the points it raises are largely taken from his earlier works and inadequately dramatized.

The main action of the novel begins with the return of Lord Ormont and his wife to England. A former military hero who fell in disgrace because of a high-handed action in the Indian War, he has married a much younger woman, Aminta, who has venerated him since her girlhood. The marriage took place on the Continent, where Ormont retired in a sulk with the English. When the couple finally return to London, Ormont, still offended, refuses to present Aminta to society as his wife, so that her position is left ambiguous; his sister consequently believes that no marriage occurred and considers her an adventuress. With Ormont's careless tolerance, Aminta gets into frivolous company and is pursued, unsuccessfully, by a predatory admirer. This episode starts to open her eyes to her husband. Meanwhile, Matey Weyburn, whom she loved during her school years, has become secretary to Lord Ormont. Their love revives but is kept under control until Lord Ormont rebuffs her wish to see the ancestral home of the Ormont family. Although Ormont subsequently repents and prepares to give Aminta her place in society, it is too late. After renouncing her marriage and rediscovering Matey's devotion, she accompanies Matey to the Continent and helps him run an international progressive school. Seven years later, Lord Ormont takes his grand-nephew to be educated there, thus signaling his forgiveness of their "offense against good citizenship."[19]

The novel reworks the situation of *The Egoist* without the intense psychological penetration and social satire combined in the study of Willoughby. Lord Ormont is a very simple character: archconservative, inarticulate, lacking in ideas, and traditional in his proprietary, condescending attitude to his wife. Characteristically he sees Aminta's bid for social recognition as an attack on his generalship and responds as if to a military campaign. But Meredith treats him gently, so that he is merely pathetic and of little consequence in the world the novel portrays. His sulking is foolish, like that of a schoolboy who cannot take a licking.

Aminta is one of Meredith's inexperienced but spunky young women whose sexual awakening is accompanied by the search for an

understanding and supportive partner. Like Emilia, Clara, Diana, and
Nesta, she has to free herself from the imprisonment of an earlier,
unsatisfactory relationship—her marriage—as well as from the egoism
of a self-pitying despair that threatens to lead her into another degrading bond. The proximity of Matey Weyburn, his actual teaching,
and his example of self-control help her not to submit to another egoistical male but to recognize her own needs. Significantly, she and
Matey declare their love only after she has independently renounced
her marriage; although they can build on the intimacy of their past,
Meredith stresses the fact that they take no undue advantage of their
situation and admit only friendship to each other until Ormont's behavior justifies Aminta's break with her husband.

Like all of Meredith's altruistic heroes, Matey is only too crystal
clear, but in the marriage and separation of Lord Ormont and
Aminta, Meredith has touched on several issues that remain blurred.
The ostensible cause of their incompatibility is Lord Ormont's unrea-
sonable refusal to give Aminta her place in society—a refusal meant
to punish the English by withholding a beautiful and talented young
woman from their social affairs, but in effect depriving Aminta of the
chance to shine in public. But one wonders why Aminta, with her
love of sports and the outdoors, would be eager to join a circle shown
throughout the novel as sterile and frivolous. A more complex question then arises: what kind of marriage has this been, in the first
place? There are hints of a mercenary intention, a poor but ambitious
young woman allying herself with a rich man looking for a decorative
"slave" (95). The May–December motif is touched upon but rejected:
Aminta does not yearn for a youthful husband. (Society, in the form
of Ormont's sister, plays up this motif, trying to explain Aminta's
attraction for the man.) On the other hand, there seems to be little
communication in this marriage; seven years of life together have not
made Aminta comfortable enough with her husband to call him by
his first name, and suddenly she discovers that "she had not known
love" (128)—the phrase is left ambiguous. It is also not clear how far
Aminta shares resentment against the British for his disgrace.

The implausibility of Lord Ormont's motives for refusing Aminta
her rightful place is the weakest spot in the novel. One might understand his reluctance to present her at Court, but to deny her even to
his sister, with whom he has kept on friendly terms, taxes one's cre-
dulity. It is equally implausible that a man so concerned with his
honor would be so careless as to leave his greatest "jewel," his wife,

exposed to slander. As Norman Kelvin has noted, the lack of plausibility in Lord Ormont's conduct damages the novel severely.[20] He is at first a sphinx to both his wife and the reader and, in the end, of little interest to either.

"The enthusiast, when not lyrical, is perilously near to boring" (152)—Meredith's gently satiric remark on the young pedagogue Matey is applicable to the novel itself. Matey's prominence allows the author to discourse on his favorite ideas directly and unironically, particularly on his military concerns and educational theories, the latter derived from his own experiences at the Moravian school at Neuwied as well as his feminist point of view. Like most of Meredith's novels, *Lord Ormont* is set in the opening years of Queen Victoria's reign, and the military discussions purportedly reflect British anxiety at that time about foreign invasions; Meredith's real concern, however, is with the nation's loss of intelligent leadership and moral fiber in the eighties and nineties. As the schoolmaster is in ascendance over the military man, so the novel itself assumes a rather schoolmasterly tone, often pontificating rather than dramatizing. "There is little pleasure to be on the lecture-rostrum for a narrator sensible to the pulses of his audience. Justice compels at times" (94), the narrator pleads. Justice compels rather often.

When he is not lecturing, Meredith is enthusiastically lyrical, glorifying outdoor life, physical activity, and the beauty of southern England. Aminta's psychological release from Lord Ormont is shown in a sequence of outdoor scenes, ending in a rapturous swim in the sea, far from land, during which she and Matey recall their childhood love while reveling in their freedom like children on holiday. A holiday spirit of great buoyancy pervades the novel. Perhaps because Matey, with his vigor and reasonableness, is so prominent and so obviously superior to Lord Ormont, one is confident from early on that Aminta's ordeal will not be excessively prolonged. Matey's own problem, his poverty, is solved by some patient waiting for an inheritance. Lord Ormont's forgiveness of the couple saves their school, sparing them any harsh consequences of their offense against social conventions. Society, in fact, becomes irrelevant to their idyll. By moving Matey and Aminta out of England—with a hint that even other continents are available if needed—Meredith adds another evasion to a novel of "difficulties unmet." It is symptomatic of a romantic vision unchecked in this work by his usual sense of social and psychological realities. One can almost hear Victor Radnor in the background: "All is coming right—must come right."

The Amazing Marriage

In his last completed novel, *The Amazing Marriage* (1895; serialized in *Scribner's Magazine,* January–December 1895), Meredith recovered a clear view of his characters, the logic of their development, and the overall design of his story. This work sums up the endeavors of his entire career: his attempt to create a new fiction for a discriminating audience; his interest in the juxtaposition of contrasts; and his plea for fellow feeling, particularly toward women. He had worked on the novel intermittently since 1879, the year of *The Egoist,* and made use of narrative strategies from as far back as *Sandra Belloni; The Amazing Marriage* can thus be seen, in essence, as a recapitulation of his life's work.

In this novel Meredith exploited an issue that had given his critics much material for hostile reviews: his avoidance of highly dramatic scenes in favor of close analysis and indirect narration. He concluded that a novel needed both, the drama of the story and the drama of internal development. In the cooperation of two narrators, a Dame Gossip who supplies the raw material of the story and a Novelist who edits it, Meredith dramatizes the possible union of two contrasting artistic attitudes—romance, in the depiction of spectacular events and larger-than-life characters, and realism.[21] The situation is more complex than in *Sandra Belloni,* where he had also used two narrators. Here the two collaborate and influence each other, the analytical Novelist predominating in the text but dependent on Dame Gossip's material and increasingly tolerant of her interruptions. In fact, he gives her the last word: "But the melancholy, the pathos of it [the story], the heart of all England stirred by it, have been . . . sacrificed in the vain effort to render events as consequent to your understanding as a piece of logic, through an exposure of character! Character must ever be a mystery, only to be explained in some degree by conduct."[22]

Dame Gossip and the Novelist, then, stand in the broadest sense for romance and realism. As Gillian Beer points out, the resulting story has both folktale charm and psychological depth, and the combination of perspectives makes the same point as the narrative itself.[23] The protagonists of this story are formed along similarly contrasting

lines: Carinthia is a simple "epic" character, whereas Lord Fleetwood
is contradictory and complex—a "morbid" character.[24] The amazing
marriage between these two does not succeed; the impact of time and
the burden of guilt unconfessed and unforgiven stand against it. The
marriage between Dame Gossip and the Novelist, on the other hand,
does succeed. In his acknowledgment of the need for incident, for romantically heightened events, for the unfathomable mystery of character, Meredith makes a tentative and qualified peace with his public.
He still gives the Novelist the bulk of the work to do because Dame
Gossip, the collective "reader" of the world's affairs, is too ready to
ascribe to the "mystery of character" what should be explored as
moral deficiencies. But he admits that romance has a place in every-
day life and a power to irradiate and transform it.

The novel begins with Dame Gossip's rambling and melodramatic
account of the heroine's parents: a story of romantic elopement and
exile, engaging the imagination and sympathies of generations and
furnishing material for numerous ballads. As in epic tradition, she
provides the heroine's illustrious ancestry. Then the Novelist takes
over, introducing Carinthia Jane Kirby as a young woman in a spe-
cific time and place (the 1830s in a mountainous Austrian province
from which she takes her name) and with a lively, engaging character.
Following her and her brother, Chillon, on their mountain walk away
from home and toward the country of their parents' birth, he displays
her love of nature, courage, practical sense, and affection for her
brother. He also indicates, through the words of a natural philosopher
whom they meet, Gower Woodseer (modeled after Robert Louis Stevenson), the fascinating quality of her appearance; Woodseer calls her
"a beautiful Gorgon—a haggard Venus" (78).

The story of Carinthia's marriage to Lord Fleetwood is truly amazing, providing many occasions for Dame Gossip's emotional interruptions. Lord Fleetwood, the richest young man in England, proposes
to her on the spur of the moment, is accepted, marries her, deserts
her on their wedding day, returns briefly to consummate the marriage, is pursued by her over several months, becomes a father, gradually rediscovers her charm, and attempts a reconciliation, but is
rebuffed and dies of self-inflicted penances in a monastery. As this
summary indicates, the novel is mostly concerned with Lord Fleetwood's development; once he has deserted Carinthia, she recedes from
the reader's view, except for a few scenes in which they meet and she
displays again her early courage, common sense, and a new and in-

creasing sophistication of speech and conduct. Except for these scenes, she is present only through the distorted view of Fleetwood's mind and through the contradictory myths created by the collective imagination of society: as a patient Griselda, a "Countess of Whitechapel," a Britomart, a modern Amazon. The reader must remember the early scenes in Austria to retain his impression of her lively personality.

The novel exploits the cliché of the opposition between nature and culture, revealing in the development of its protagonists the fallacy of this convention. Through the juxtaposition of the mountain walk and the gambling scene at Baden, where Carinthia first meets her compatriots, the reader is initially tempted to accept the cliché; even in style, Meredith plays up the contrast, as Gillian Beer has pointed out.[25] Fleetwood falls under Carinthia's spell because she differs from the women he has known. In his first enchantment, he thinks of her as "a noble daughter of the woods"(121). In effect, he engages himself to a symbol rather than to a living person with social as well as natural dimensions. Such an act leads inevitably to disillusionment, as it does for Fleetwood on his wedding day, when he finds out that his bride is unsophisticated and barely able to speak English. Meredith underscores the childlike simplicity of the young woman to suggest the folly and self-indulgence in Fleetwood's idealization of her.

In the course of the novel, it becomes apparent that the dichotomy of nature and culture is of Fleetwood's own making, related to the division in his psychological makeup. As the richest man in England, he has limitless resources to indulge himself and has learned, in doing so, the hollowness of this pleasure. Like Victor Radnor, he is too fortunate for his own good. Because he finds that he can buy his friends, he despises them, and life's main challenge to him lies in his seeing how far he can corrupt them. But his intermittent patronage of Gower Woodseer points to another side in him contrasted with his cynicism: he yearns for something to look up to, for clear, unequivocal moral integrity in another person.[26] Frustrated in this search, he indulges in a specious Byronism, designed mainly to set him off from the contemptible rest of the world and composed of a sentimental nature worship and a rigid fidelity to his word once given. Out of these impulses, true and specious, he enters into marriage, without realizing that the spiritual challenge that would give shape and meaning to his life is right before him in the person of his wife and in the psychological consequences of their union.

For consequences there are, and not just in the surprising birth of his child. During a quick, surreptitious visit to his wife on their wedding night, Fleetwood has experienced the beauty of Carinthia's wholehearted love ("Love had eyes, love had a voice that night" [222]), and no subsequent act of hers can quite efface this impact. He has come with the sadistic intention of making her another victim of his "devilry," and he leaves partly overcome by the depth of her feelings. Because he would like to blot out what seems to him a defeat, the scene appears only in fragmentary and vague hints.[27] Meredith thus suggests that it is Fleetwood's reaction to it, not the scene itself, that is important—his panicked attempt to pretend that nothing of consequence has happened and his secret thrilled recognition that something has. From now on, Carinthia becomes the standard by which to measure others, particularly women, and the hidden spur to measure himself against her. The novel very convincingly traces his progress toward recognition of her personality, which gradually converts him from a sadistic monster into a complex, not unsympathetic man. But as in many of Meredith's protagonists, his change is not complete. His habit of despising his fellowmen makes it impossible for him to open himself entirely to his wife, even though he now worships her—total confession, he thinks, must be reserved for the church alone. Thus she hears from elsewhere how he has schemed to damage her brother, and this act, rather than his earlier mistreatment of her, she cannot forgive.

For Carinthia the obvious result of the wedding night is her pregnancy and motherhood. As mother of the Fleetwood heir she assumes, of course, an important position implicitly recognized by her husband. But her motherhood does not circumscribe the growth of her personality. She develops in many areas, revealing more and more the qualities of a natural leader and a sophisticated lady.[28] Isolation from her husband inevitably shifts her love away from him to her child and her brother. Her idealization of Chillon, who is not as disinterested a brother as she imagines, constitutes a blindness easily explained by the ignorance and dependency of her youth. Here, through some generosity of his own, Fleetwood might have advanced his own cause with her. But a complicating factor in the Chillon-Carinthia-Fleetwood triangle is the fact that Chillon's wife, Henrietta, had been unsuccessfully courted by Fleetwood before he met Carinthia. Some remaining desire for Henrietta and a fierce jealousy of Chillon, whom he also correctly accuses of having partly engineered his own marriage to Carinthia, combine in his nasty schemes to undermine Chillon's career and marriage. Because Henrietta is a weak, pleasure-seeking woman, he almost succeeds. That Chillon and Henrietta are deeply implicated in the Fleetwood tragedy is one of Meredith's most skillful strokes in the novel, providing additional motives for Fleetwood's apparently inexplicable behavior and commenting on a society in which women, by being confined to a merely ornamental function, can ruin themselves and their men.

Close to the end of the novel, Meredith adds another skillful stroke: he brings Carinthia back before the reader. For a long time she has been a remote, even mythical figure, awe inspiring even to Fleetwood in his few encounters with her, for example, when she single-handedly holds a rabid dog at bay. In the last two chapters she is again vividly present, as she was in the scenes before her marriage. She is humanized, and her "epic" character reveals complex feelings toward her husband, her brother, and her sister-in-law. It is important that the reader see her again as an individual and not share the error of Fleetwood, whose blindness to her emotions at their last meeting prevents him from expressing, and thus purifying, his own. Meredith suggests that even in his final worship of Carinthia Fleetwood's attitude is ultimately reductive—an idealization disregarding the reality of her character, her emotions, and her potentialities. Because he cannot genuinely appreciate the aptness of Gower Woodseer's paradoxical description of Carinthia—"a beautiful Gorgon—a haggard Venus"—he misses out on the romance Meredith finds in a true meeting of spirits.

The Amazing Marriage dramatizes and clarifies Meredith's idea that romance, in life and in art, can never be divorced from reality if it is to be of more than transient value. Meredith makes use of the conventional trappings of the romance—amazing events, heightened characters, even exotic places (Austria and Wales)—and displays in Fleetwood's worship of Nature and Self a "romantic" attitude the reader is tempted to share, since the story withholds, for a long time, the corrective vision of Carinthia as a real woman. In the subplot of Dame Gossip and the Novelist's tense collaboration, however, Meredith provides a guide to the reader. Without dismissing the claims of romance, he indicates its proper place in life and art. Dame Gossip makes much of the "melancholy, the pathos" of Carinthia's and Fleetwood's story; but this melancholy and pathos touch us only because both Carinthia and Fleetwood are under the Novelist's scrutiny as living, complex characters.

Character may always be a mystery, as the Dame asserts. But where fruitful relations between the sexes are concerned, the romantic flight into "mystery of character," by which one evades, like Fleetwood, the reality of one's obligations and misreads the reality of one's partner, proves ultimately futile. The romance of life, Meredith argues in all his work, derives from a deep understanding of reality. In *The Amazing Marriage* he extends his argument: where fiction is meant to enlarge insight and charity, romance has a permanent place only when the Novelist can enter into the mystery of character and make it come to life for the reader. Meredith's last novel thus offers a final statement on his art, reaffirming his lifelong attempt to join romance and realism in a paradoxical and precarious embrace.

Chapter Six
Conclusion

Reading Meredith is an often exhilarating and equally often disturbing experience. His poems and novels vividly reflect the assumptions, inherent contradictions, and developing conflicts of the Victorian age. Spread over a period of creativity of more than fifty years, they combine, in uneasy juxtaposition and varying emphasis, the rational outlook of the pre-Victorians Fielding and Peacock, the "natural supernaturalism" of Carlyle and his romantic predecessors both English and German, the moral urgency of the liberal reformers, the skeptical intelligence and irony of Thackeray, and the buoyant spirit of the neoromantics like Robert Louis Stevenson. One is tempted to add the preciosity of the Pre-Raphaelites and the extravagant satirical wit of Oscar Wilde. Of these contrasting elements, Meredith managed to create a substantial and significant body of work, always provocative and, to this day, controversial.

In his appeal for self-knowledge, self-discipline, and charity Meredith seems the quintessential Victorian novelist, committed to a realistic picture of human nature and society and to the improvement of life through his art. But his novels also test the limits of realistic fiction. In his late work, particularly, his mistrust of rhetorical and narrative conventions, his pervasive irony, and his deliberate intellectual elitism seem to work against the appeal for communality characteristic of Victorian fiction, in fact to point toward the modern novel. It is significant that such diverse twentieth-century novelists as Virginia Woolf, James Joyce, and André Gide have explicitly acknowledged their debt to Meredith, even while noting his flaws as an artist.[1] Today Meredith remains a problematic literary figure: too complex, allusive, and ironic to be the typical Victorian "sage," yet too insistent, opinionated, and hearty to be the modern intellectual.

In 1897 Arthur Symons wrote in the *Fortnightly Review:* "*The Tragic Comedians,* which is the title of one of Mr. Meredith's novels, might well be applied to the whole series. So picturesquely, under the light of so sharp a paradox, does he conceive of human existence."[2] Another title equally applicable to Meredith's novels is "The Amazing Marriage." As Symons and other contemporary critics realized, Meredith constantly and deliberately joined contrasting elements in both his poetry and his prose and did so with a panache amazing to his readers. He combined comedy and tragedy, fiction and analysis, irony and symbolism, realism and romance. In his poetry he used prose elements such as conversational dramatic monologue, and "Modern Love" approaches the "novel in verse" like Robert Browning's *The Ring and the Book*. On the other hand, his prose fiction works by implication and condensation more often characteristic of poetry, incorporating a profusion of imagery while disregarding plot except as it is refracted through the consciousness of his characters.

Meredith saw himself as a realist, following and improving upon Thackeray. More insistently than his predecessor he drew attention to the paradox that "realistic fiction" constitutes—the contradiction inherent in this concept. His novels deny his readers the pleasure of immersion in an imaginative world. Meredith constantly stresses the fictionality of his characters—explicitly, through the nominal presence of "novelists" or editors who ostensibly create the novel, and implicitly, through literary parody and allusion. In addition, he omits the physical details of a setting except as they bear on or symbolize his characters' emotional lives. Finally, he presents the events of a story in individual scenes, often without obvious connections; it is the reader's task to link them by noting how they subsequently affect the characters.[3] The Meredithian commentary accompanying or following each scene destroys the illusion of reality and challenges us to scrutinize motives and acts, to penetrate to levels of subconsciousness accessible only through symbol and myth, without ever entirely abandoning our critical stance. Each scene becomes an essay involving character, author, and reader in multiple ironies—the whole designed, perhaps more than anything else, to show the difficulty of ascertaining and conveying truth through conventional methods.

Besides "the amazing marriage" two other metaphors serve to illustrate Meredith's experimental and problematic art. One recurrent figure is that of the knight-errant who champions a noble cause but has to learn—and often fails to—that chivalry can be tainted by an egoism destructive to its aim. The danger inherent in knight-errantry is to see the world in black and white, in fixed categories and abstractions, and to act on rigid principles that, however noble, ultimately prevent the hero from acquiring self-knowledge. Meredith himself espoused and energetically pursued a variety of causes in his novels: the emancipation of women and the lower classes, a more responsible aristocracy, a fairer distribution of wealth, better national defenses, better schools, Irish Home Rule—the list could go on to include even such trivia as vegetarianism and fresh air for babies. In his rather strident clamor for practical reforms, in his often sentimental praise of women as "Nature's own," and in his categorizing of national qualities by spurious ethnological theories, Meredith himself sometimes appears today slightly ludicrous. As the knight-errant championing a literature in advance of its time and proclaiming repeatedly his disenchantment with the contemporary reader, he risks being suspected of special pleading.

Set against the metaphor of knight-errantry in the novels is the equally pervasive image of the sea, symbolizing the unpredictable flow of reality.[4] In Meredith's work as a whole this juxtaposition also applies. Beside Meredith the crusader and social reformer is Meredith the relativist, the ironist, and the psychologist. In his poems he celebrates and conveys change, movement, the never-ceasing energy of Nature. In his novels many levels of awareness come alive, momentarily fusing, then separating, coloring one another, and then combining in a different mode or with a different emphasis. Used by a character to shore up his defenses against uncomfortable insight, words reveal a slippery multiplicity of meanings spilling over into the narrative itself and the authorial commentary; language, seemingly taking on a life of its own, exposes both logic and convention as inadequate to the rendering of psychological experience. Meredith's constant shifts of perspective, reflected in the modulations of tone to express the individual thought patterns and fluctuating levels of awareness in his characters, often leave the reader floundering, bewildered by the lack of a firm line between fact and figure of speech, yet impressed by the writer's skill in navigating what still remains recognizably a story.

Meredith's extraordinary attempts to trace the desires, fears, evasions, and self-delusions of the mind down to their roots in the subconscious and his un-Victorian willingness to grant both men and women irrepressible sexual instincts point toward D. H. Lawrence. His technical experiments with language, his shifts in perspective, his approximation of stream of consciousness in the late novels, and his exploitation of paradox make him a forerunner of James Joyce.[5] In the "library" chapter of *Ulysses,* Joyce actually quotes Meredith's definition of the sentimentalist as one "who would enjoy without incurring the immense debtorship for a thing done," Sir Austin Feverel's most famous epigram. It is significant that Joyce selected this particular quotation; the twentieth-century novelist obviously felt that his affinity with Meredith was less in the brilliance of verbal art than in the commitment to an unsentimental rendition of human life.

For Meredith this commitment, however much he infringed upon it in practice, was an almost religious obligation. Sentimentality and hypocrisy he considered the refined versions of an egoism that man, in the dawn of his race, had needed to survive but that had no place in the modern world. That Victorian society was riddled with both flaws indicated to him—as it did to his contemporary Matthew Arnold—the thinness of civilization's veneer. "We are barbarians," says Dr. Middleton in *The Egoist* (2:257), "on a forcing soil of wealth, in a conservatory of comfortable security; but still barbarians." Again and again, Meredith suggests that wealth and comfortable security may in themselves retard the advent of the truly civilized citizen. He did not doubt, however, that man could transform his egoism into a socially beneficial quality and would, over the long run of evolution, do so.

Because Meredith firmly believed in the ultimate benevolence of Nature and in human civilization as part of this Nature, he did not share the anxiety, the melancholy, or the profound sense of human limitations one finds in Thackeray and many of the late Victorians. He was a relativist in that he recognized the folly of fixed positions in the flux of life, but as his poetry shows, his relativism stopped when he contemplated Nature herself. And although he treated ironically the society of his age and his country, he was fiercely committed to the idea of society; he championed women's emancipation and self-assertion only insofar as they would lead to a healthier community. In Meredith's work the single life, whether ascetic or self-indulgent, is presented as incomplete and wasteful; self-sufficiency is an illusion, and mature people get married. It is true that toward the end of his career Meredith was no longer able to envision a satisfactory marriage in any but vague symbolic terms (Nesta and Dartrey in *One of Our Conquerors*, Carinthia and Owain Wythan in *The Amazing Marriage*), and he recorded the dangers of his age—individual and collective madness through self-centeredness—with a sometimes inartistic passion. Yet the idea to which he always returned and which never fails to give buoyancy to his novels is that Nature's unalterable laws will ultimately take care of human follies.

Meredith and his well-adjusted heroes look back to the past only to draw lessons from it; they turn to Nature only to renew their energies for social service; they marry and have families not to indulge in, or flee into, domestic idylls but to support each other in their work for the common good; and they foster wit, education, and the appreciation of art to make themselves more fit to advance the species. They accept their roles in life cheerfully because their larger vision embraces the development of a more glorious race. Meredith, it has been said, always retained the outlook of a youth for whom the future has a limitless romantic appeal. And unlike Thomas Hardy, he was convinced of a universe evolving according to consistent laws that man could understand and obey. Whereas for Hardy altruistic service merely alleviated the suffering of man under the careless and chaotic sway of chance, for Meredith its benefits in the present laid the foundations for future blessings.

In this worldview genuine tragedy is not possible. But several of Meredith's characters approach tragic stature, and others, such as Nevil Beauchamp and Diana Warwick, are prevented from reaching it only because of the arbitrariness of Meredith's plots. Meredith, it appears, cannot let tragedy happen except as instances of folly which, he implies, could have been avoided had the protagonists, their educators, and society as a whole been more reasonable. But in novel after novel he draws "what is false within" with a persuasiveness, consistency, and power of figurative language that suggest the inevitability of a tragic outcome and hint at the existence of real evil in the universe. And it is this uneasy suggestion, coupled with a fierce determination to keep an unmistakably discordant element within the framework of an optimistic worldview, that continues to impress and fascinate the reader.

In one of his reviews of *The Egoist* W. E. Henley said of Meredith: "He writes with the pen of a great artist in his left hand and the razor of a spiritual suicide in his right."[6] Most of his critics, contemporary and later, have detected greatness in his spirit rather than his art. Robert Louis Stevenson, Henry James, Thomas Hardy, and Oscar Wilde were ambivalent in their praise of his artistic achievement.[7] Henry James in particular found Meredith's insistence on philosophy in fiction, his apparently willful dislocation of plot, and his verbal extravagance hard to tolerate. "The artist," James declared, "was nothing to the good citizen and the liberalized bourgeois."[8] And in 1910, Percy Lubbock, reviewing Meredith's *Collected Works,* pointed out that "the single-minded attitude of the artist before his work, his homage to it and it alone" was wanting.[9]

Meredith was not interested in a single-minded attitude, whether private or professional; single-mindedness, he believed, too often betrayed an egoistical narrowness likely to result in spiritual atrophy. Clearly speaking for the author, his heroine Diana Warwick says, "I thank God I'm at war with myself" (*Diana,* 48). War, battle, strife— these metaphors apply to Meredith's novels as well as to his dialectical worldview. The reader, also, has to do battle when he takes on this demanding, opinionated, yet paradoxical writer and consents to be "thwacked with a fantastical delivery of the verities" (*Belloni,* 2:230). Our enjoyment of Meredith's poems and novels derives from the encounter with a large, vigorous spirit, whose commitment to the truth of human experience—both the reality of its transitoriness and the romance of its aspirations—continues to speak to us over the years.

Notes and References

Preface

1. Virginia Woolf, "The Novels of George Meredith," in *The Second Common Reader* (1932; reprint, New York, 1960), 213.

Chapter One

1. Edward Clodd, "George Meredith: Some Recollections," *Fortnightly Review* 86 (July-December 1909):20.
2. Meredith called his father "a muddler and a fool." See Clodd, "Recollections," 20. Contact between father and son remained slight, even after Augustus had returned to England from South Africa, and even though Augustus greatly admired his writer son. Augustus felt personally hurt by the portrait of Evan Harrington, the socially ambitious tailor's son.
3. Lady Butcher [Alice Brandreth], *Memories of George Meredith, O.M.* (New York: Scribner's, 1919), 33.
4. Lionel Stevenson, *The Ordeal of George Meredith: A Biography* (New York, 1953), 8.
5. According to Constantin Photiadès, as late as 1908 Meredith insisted that he was "pure Celt." See Constantin Photiadès, *George Meredith: His Life, Genius, and Teaching*, trans. Arthur Price (1913; reprint, Port Washington, N.Y.: Kennikat Press, 1970), 12. For a corrective view, see Stevenson, *Ordeal*, 7.
6. Stevenson, *Ordeal*, 11.
7. See Stevenson, *Ordeal*, 16–18, for speculations about this undocumented period in Meredith's life.
8. In one of the very few remarks Meredith made later about his marriage, he exaggerated the difference in age: "No sun warmed my roof-tree; the marriage was a blunder; she was nine years my senior." Cited in Clodd, "Recollections," 21.
9. For Meredith's relationship with Thomas Love Peacock (1785–1866), novelist, poet, friend of Shelley, and official of the East India Company (from which he had long retired when the Merediths came to live with him), see J. L. Madden, *Thomas Love Peacock* (London: Evans Brothers, 1967), 30ff., and Stevenson, *Ordeal*, 23, 42–45.
10. The book did receive a few fairly positive reviews. See Ioan Williams, ed., *Meredith: The Critical Heritage* (New York, 1971), 40–42, and L. T. Hergenhan, "The Reception of George Meredith's Early Novels," *Nineteenth-Century Fiction* 19 (1964):213–35.

11. C. L. Cline, ed., *The Letters of George Meredith*, (Oxford, 1970), 1:124–25; hereafter cited in the text as *Letters*.

12. See Stevenson, *Ordeal*, 64, for more autobiographical details.

13. Francis Burnand, *Records and Reminiscences* (London, 1904). Cited in S. M. Ellis, *George Meredith: His Life and Friends in Relation to His Work* (New York: Dodd, Mead, 1920), 107.

14. Lady Butcher, *Memories*, 2.

15. Ibid., 55.

16. Cited in Stevenson, *Ordeal*, 294.

17. Photiadès, *George Meredith*, 9.

18. See Stevenson, *Ordeal*, 321, as well as the reviews in the *Pall Mall Gazette* 61 (December 1895) and the *Spectator* 76 (January 1896) cited in Williams, ed., *Critical Heritage*, 442 and 452, respectively.

19. Meredith transferred publishing rights in America from Roberts Brothers in Boston to Scribner's, who proceeded to bring out a collected edition of Meredith's novels in the United States concurrently with the one brought out by Constable in England.

20. Henry James, Letter to Edmund Gosse, 11 October 1912, in *The Letters of Henry James*, ed. Percy Lubbock (London: Macmillan, 1920), 2:261.

21. Desmond MacCarthy, *Portraits* (1932; reprint, New York: Oxford University Press, 1955), 171–72.

22. Photiadès, "A Visit to Flint Cottage, 22 September 1908," in *George Meredith*, 3.

Chapter Two

1. For a discussion of Meredith's collections and their publishing history, see Phyllis B. Bartlett, introduction to *The Poems of George Meredith* (New Haven, 1978), 1:xxvii–xl. All quotations from poems are taken from this edition and are cited in the text by stanza and line.

2. For recent studies and comments on Meredith's poetry, see John Lucas, "Meredith as Poet," in *Meredith Now: Some Critical Essays*, ed. Ian Fletcher (New York, 1971), 14–33; Carol Bernstein, *Precarious Enchantment: A Reading of Meredith's Poetry* (Washington, D.C., 1979); Wendell Harris, "Sifting and Sorting Meredith's Poetry," in *The Victorian Experience: The Poets*, ed. Richard A. Levine (Athens, Ohio, 1982), 115–37; Keith Hanley, Introduction to *George Meredith: Selected Poems* (Manchester: Carcanet Press, 1983).

3. George M. Trevelyan, *The Poetry and Philosophy of George Meredith* (London: Constable, 1906), 64.

4. Meredith was first charged with this fault by Charles Kingsley, in "This Year's Song-Crop," *Fraser's Magazine* 44 (December 1851). Cited in M. Buxton Forman, *George Meredith: Some Early Appreciations* (London: Chapman & Hall, 1909), 18–19.

5. For Meredith's closeness to the ideas of Lamarck, see Norman Kelvin, *A Troubled Eden: Nature and Society in the Works of George Meredith* (Stanford, Calif., 1961), 117.

6. See Lucas, "Meredith as Poet," 21–22; Bernstein, *Precarious Enchantment*, 53–55, 59–62.

7. Patricia Crunden, "The Woods of Westermain," *Victorian Poetry* 5, no. 4 (Winter 1967):265–82, and Bernstein, *Precarious Enchantment*, 146–48, discuss the interaction between structure and message in "The Woods of Westermain" in greater detail.

8. For an excellent discussion of Meredith's diction and imagery, see Bernstein, "Style: The Language of Quality," in *Precarious Enchantment*.

9. The comparison was first made by John Bailey, "The Poetry of George Meredith," *Fortnightly Review*, n.s. 86 (July 1909):42.

10. Following Meredith himself, I use the term *sonnet* for the individual poems in "Modern Love."

11. For a discussion of the topicality of "Modern Love" and its relation to the Renaissance sonnet cycles, see Arlene Golden, " 'The Game of Sentiment': Tradition and Innovation in Meredith's 'Modern Love,' " *ELH* 40 (1973):264–84. Dorothy Mermin examines its fictional strategies and its novelistic conventions in "Poetry as Fiction: Meredith's *Modern Love*," *ELH* 43 (1976):100–119.

12. See Willie Reader, "The Autobiographical Author as Fictional Character: Point of View in Meredith's 'Modern Love,' " *Victorian Poetry* 10 (1972):132. Bernstein, *Precarious Enchantment*, 176 n. 4, also suggests this possibility.

13. See Lucas, "Meredith as Poet," 23, for the unusual view that the "inanities" of sonnet 50 demonstrate Meredith's deliberately satirical treatment of the narrator.

14. Norman Friedman, "The Jangled Harp: Symbolic Structure in 'Modern Love,' " *Modern Language Quarterly* 18 (March 1957):9–26.

15. Cited in Williams, ed., *Critical Heritage*, 98.

Chapter Three

1. *The Ordeal of Richard Feverel* (New York: Scribner's, 1909), 226. Citations in the text are to this edition.

2. Judith Wilt, *The Readable People of George Meredith* (Princeton, 1975), 51–80.

3. See *Sandra Belloni* (New York: Scribner's, 1910), 1:113, where he contrasts Thackeray's "puppetry" with his own. Citations in the text are to this edition. See also Gillian Beer, *Meredith: A Change of Masks* (London, 1970), 38.

4. *The Shaving of Shagpat: An Arabian Entertainment* (New York: Scribner's, 1909), 3.

5. J. McKechnie, *Meredith's Allegory, The Shaving of Shagpat, Interpreted* (1910; reprint, London: Folcroft Library Editions, 1976). In a letter to McKechnie (*Letters*, 3:1559) Meredith implies that *Shagpat* is an allegory.

6. Preface to *The Shaving of Shagpat*, 2d ed. (1865), in M. Buxton Forman, *A Bibliography of the Writings in Prose and Verse of George Meredith* (Edinburgh, 1922), 15.

7. See Fletcher, "*The Shaving of Shagpat*: Meredith's Comic Apocalypse," in *Meredith Now*, 34–68, for a discussion of literary and autobiographical sources and influences.

8. Joseph Moses, *The Novelist as Comedian: George Meredith and the Ironic Sensibility* (New York, 1983), 95 ff., discusses the function of irony in *Shagpat* as the "comedy of Meaning."

9. See Beer, *Change of Masks*, 28–29, for changes in the second edition (1878). Like most critics I base my discussion on the 1878 version.

10. For *Richard Feverel* as a bildungsroman and its relation to Rousseau's theories, see Juliet Mitchell, "*The Ordeal of Richard Feverel*: A Sentimental Education," in Fletcher, ed., *Meredith Now*, 68–94. See also Jerome Buckley, *Season of Youth: The Bildungsroman from Dickens to Golding* (Cambridge, Mass., 1974), 63–82.

11. Beer, *Change of Masks*, 23–24.

12. Ibid., 33.

13. See, for instance, the review by Samuel Lucas in the *Times* (London), 14 October 1859, cited in Williams, ed., *Critical Heritage*, 82–83.

14. An extended study of Adrian relates him to the novel's subplot in Wilt, *The Readable People*, 86–116.

15. Saturday Review, 9 July 1859, cited in Williams, ed., *Critical Heritage*, 71–76.

16. *Evan Harrington* (New York: Scribner's, 1910), 232. Citations in the text are to this edition.

17. See Jack Lindsay, *George Meredith: His Life and Work* (London, 1956). For an effective rebuttal of Lindsay's argument concerning *Evan Harrington*, see J. M. S. Tomkins, "On Re-reading *Evan Harrington*," in Fletcher, ed., *Meredith Now*, 119–21.

18. See Margaret Tarratt, " 'Snips,' 'Snobs,' and the 'True Gentleman' in *Evan Harrington*," in Fletcher, ed., *Meredith Now*, 99–101.

19. John Cardinal Newman, "The Idea of a University," in *English Prose of the Victorian Era* ed. C. F. Harrold and W. D. Templeman (New York: Oxford University Press, 1974), 610.

20. Beer, *Change of Masks*, 44.

21. As Judith Wilt observes, "The inflated metaphor is the sentimentality of the imaginative soul, the hippogriff of the artist" (*The Readable People*, 145).

22. Lionel Stevenson, "Meredith's Atypical Novel: A Study of *Rhoda Fleming*," in *The Image of the Work: Essays in Criticism*, ed. B. H. Lehman (Berkeley: University of California Press, 1955), 89–109.

23. *Rhoda Fleming* (New York: Scribner's, 1910), 125.

24. David Howard, "*Rhoda Fleming*: Meredith in the Margin," in Fletcher, ed., *Meredith Now*, 133–34.

25. Meredith used the terms *morbid* and *epic* in a letter to Frederick Maxse, 28 December 1865 (*Letters* 1:321–22), in an attempt to explain his affinities and fascination with Hawthorne.

26. Ioan Williams, "Emilia in England and Italy," in Fletcher, ed., *Meredith Now*, 151 ff.

27. *Athenaeum*, no. 2052 (23 February 1867), cited in Williams, ed., *Critical Heritage*, 153.

28. *Saturday Review* 23 (2 February 1867), cited in Williams, ed., *Critical Heritage*, 151.

29. See Meredith's letter to Algernon C. Swinburne, 2 March 1867 (*Letters*, 1:353–54).

Chapter Four

1. For *The Satirist*, see Beer, *Change of Masks*, 115; for *The Sentimentalists*, see Stevenson, *The Ordeal of George Meredith*, 335–36. Meredith's novellas are *The House on the Beach*, *The Case of General Ople and Lady Camper*, and *The Tale of Chloe*. The first two were published serially in the *New Quarterly Magazine* during 1877, and the third one, in 1879 in the same periodical. (Meredith had also published *Farina: A Legend of Cologne* [1857], exploiting his knowledge of the Rhineland, the public's love of historical romance, and his recent critical success with *The Shaving of Shagpat*.) In the two novellas of 1877, Meredith anticipates *The Egoist* in his merciless pursuit of human folly; in *The Tale of Chloe*, he presents the quixotic self-sacrifice of a young woman in the midst of Regency high life. None of these works is distinguished by artistic excellence.

2. *Diana of the Crossways* (New York: Scribner's, 1910), 478. Citations in the text are to this edition.

3. *Essay: On the Idea of Comedy and the Uses of the Comic Spirit* (New York: Scribner's, 1910), 3. Citations in the text are to this edition.

4. Moses, *The Novelist as Comedian*, 220, stresses the importance of this passage for Meredith's aesthetics.

5. Dorothy van Ghent, *The English Novel: Form and Function* (New York, 1953), 11.

6. See Beer, *Change of Masks*, 45, for picaresque early versions of the novel.

7. *The Adventures of Harry Richmond* (New York: Scribner's, 1910), 1:14. Citations in the text are to this edition.

8. Beer, *Change of Masks*, 57.

9. See *Letters*, 1:333, 368, 411–12, 425, 450; 2:588.

10. For the influence of Goethe, see Margaret Tarratt, "*The Adventures of Harry Richmond: Bildungsroman* and the Historical Novel," in Fletcher, ed., *Meredith Now*, 169 ff.

11. For Meredith's reluctance to write a "condition of England" novel, see *Letters*, 1:432, and Norman Kelvin's rather speculative discussion in *A Troubled Eden*, 83 ff.

12. *Beauchamp's Career* (New York: Scribner's, 1910), 1:38–39.

13. For Meredith's attitude toward Carlyle in *Beauchamp's Career* and elsewhere, see John Morris, "*Beauchamp's Career*: Meredith's Acknowledgment of His Debt to Carlyle," in *Studies in Honor of John C. Hodges and Alwin Thayer*, ed. Richard B. Davis and John L. Liersay (Knoxville: University of Tennessee Press, 1961), 101–8, and Beer, *Change of Masks*, 79–80.

14. For a Marxist interpretation of Beauchamp's death, see Lindsay, *George Meredith*, 220, and Arnold Kettle, "*Beauchamp's Career*," in Fletcher, ed., *Meredith Now*, 199.

15. See Wilt, *The Readable People*, 149, 169–79.

16. *The Egoist* (New York: Scribner's, 1910), 1:6. Citations in the text are to this edition.

17. Cited in Stevenson, *The Ordeal of George Meredith*, 245. See also Angus Wilson, Afterword, to *The Egoist* (New York: Signet, 1963), 503–5, and van Ghent, *The English Novel*, 183–94, for comments on Sir Willoughby as a victim of Meredith's contempt.

18. James Moffat, *George Meredith: A Primer to the Novels* (1909; reprint, New York: Kennikat Press, 1969), 278.

19. *The Tragic Comedians* (New York: Scribner's, 1910), 112. Citations in the text are to this edition.

20. Leonée Ormond, "*The Tragic Comedians*: Meredith's Use of Image Patterns," in Fletcher, ed., *Meredith Now*, 240–43.

21. Siegfried Sassoon, *Meredith* (London: Viking, 1948), 157–58; Kelvin, *A Troubled Eden*, 112.

22. See Stevenson, *The Ordeal of George Meredith*, 254–55.

23. Meredith's portrait of Diana as a "new Woman" is briefly discussed in Lloyd Fernando, "*New Women*" in the Late Victorian Novel (University Park: Pennsylvania State University Press, 1977), 71–72.

24. Beer, *Change of Masks*, 160–64, puts the case gently. For a more trenchant verdict, see Donald D. Stone, *Novelists in a Changing World: Meredith, James, and the Transformation of English Fiction in the 1880s* (Cambridge, Mass., 1972), 145–54.

Chapter Five

1. For a summary of the social crisis in England during the 1880s, see Stone, *Novelists in a Changing World*, 9–16; for Meredith's interest in ety-

mology, semantics, and rhetoric, see Margaret Harris, Editor's Introduction to *One of Our Conquerors* (St. Lucia, Queensland, 1975). Citations in the text are to this excellent edition.

2. D. S. Austin, "Meredith on the Nature of Metaphor," *University of Toronto Quarterly* 27 (1957): 96–101.

3. See particularly the letters to Hilda de Longueuil (*Letters*, 2:878–79) and to Lady Ulrica Duncombe (*Letters*, 3:1413, 1438–39). On Meredith's feminism, see Fernando, *"New Women"*, 70–74; Gail Cunningham, *The New Woman and the Victorian Novel* (London: Macmillan, 1978), 119 ff.

4. *Times* (London), 18 May 1891, cited in Williams, ed., *Critical Heritage*, 352.

5. *Saturday Review* 71 (23 May 1891), cited in Williams, ed., *Critical Heritage*, 352.

6. *Spectator* 66 (30 May 1891), cited in Williams, ed., *Critical Heritage*, 359–60.

7. Sassoon, *Meredith*, 208. Stone, in *Novelists in a Changing World*, 158–70, makes a convincing case for the problematic success of the novel.

8. See Beer, in *"One of Our Conquerors*: Language and Music," in Fletcher, ed., *Meredith Now*, 266: "*One of Our Conquerors* is, self-consciously, a novel *about* language and the limits of language." I am much indebted to this incisive essay. See also Moses, *The Novelist as Comedian*, 205 ff.

9. Wilt, *The Readable People*, 194 ff., shows this side of Victor with particular reference to the ineffectiveness of his friend Colney Durance, a confirmed pessimist.

10. Beer, in Fletcher, ed., *Meredith Now*, 271, points out Nataly's flaw, her dread of facing facts, and her consequent mute withdrawal from her family. In the early novel *Vittoria*, Meredith had already drawn a heroine who refuses to help her husband by speaking out about his delusions.

11. There is a striking parallel between Nataly's suffering and that of Arthur Dimmesdale in Hawthorne's *The Scarlet Letter*. Meredith was much impressed with Hawthorne and recognized artistic affinities (see letter to Maxse, 28 December 1865 [*Letters*, 1:322–23]).

12. Joseph Warren Beach, *The Comic Spirit in George Meredith* (London: Longmans, Green, 1911), 120–21, emphasizes this point.

13. For a fuller discussion of this episode, see Donald Swanson, *Three Conquerors: Character and Method in the Mature Works of George Meredith* (The Hague, 1969), 120 ff.

14. The first sentence has been analyzed by Margaret Harris, " 'The Fraternity of Old Lamps': Some Observations on George Meredith's Prose Style," *Style* 7, no. 1 (1973):271–93; Moses, *The Novelist as Comedian*, 193; and Phyllis Bartlett, "The Novels of George Meredith," *Review of English Literature* 3 (January 1962):31–46.

15. See Beer, in Fletcher, ed., *Meredith Now*, for the importance of Colney Durance's satire on languages and the role of music in this novel.

16. *Literary Review*, 8 September 1895, cited in Williams, ed., *Critical Heritage*, 409.

17. Cited in Williams, ed., *Critical Heritage*, 406–7.

18. See Barbara Hardy, in *"Lord Ormont and His Aminta* and *The Amazing Marriage,"* in Fletcher, ed., *Meredith Now*, 295–312; Kelvin, *A Troubled Eden*, 180 ff.; and Cunningham, *The New Woman*, 130–31.

19. *Lord Ormont and His Aminta* (New York: Scribner's, 1910), 332. Citations in the text are to this edition.

20. Kelvin, *A Troubled Eden*, 182–85.

21. See Wilt, *The Readable People*, 210 ff., and Beer, *Change of Masks*, 172 ff., for extended discussions on the relationship between the two narrators and their story.

22. *The Amazing Marriage* (New York: Scribner's, 1910), 510–11. Citations in the text are to this edition.

23. Beer, *Change of Masks*, 168–69.

24. Meredith uses these terms in his letter to Maxse about his affinity with Hawthorne (*Letters*, 1:322–23).

25. Beer, *Change of Masks*, 174–75. Beer notes that the style of individual passages is usually expressive of the observer's mind; in his view of the gambling halls, Gower Woodseer himself is affected by the false dichotomy.

26. For the link between Woodseer and Fleetwood, hinted at in their names, see Moses, *The Novelist as Comedian*, 62, and Wilt, *The Readable People*, 216.

27. The *Pall Mall Gazette* 61 (23 December 1895) spoke for many readers when it called the appearance of the baby "a deeply interesting case of spontaneous generation" (Williams, ed., *Critical Heritage*, 442), but there are hints enough of Fleetwood's "devilry," starting with chapter 17.

28. Barbara Hardy rightly insists on Carinthia's growth in sophistication (Fletcher, ed., *Meredith Now*, 307); this, along with her original romantic appeal, attracts Fleetwood to her anew.

Chapter Six

1. Virginia Woolf, "The Novels of George Meredith," in *The Second Common Reader* (New York, 1960), 204–13; James Joyce, "Walter Jerrold's George Meredith," in *The Critical Writings of James Joyce*, ed. Ellsworth Mason and Richard Ellmann (1959; reprint, New York: Viking, 1964), 88; *The Journals of André Gide*, trans. Justin O'Brien (New York: Knopf, 1948), 2:229.

2. Cited in Williams, ed., *Critical Heritage*, 461.

3. See E. M. Forster for a related discussion of Meredith's plots, in *Aspects of the Novel* (1927; reprint, New York: Harcourt, Brace, 1955), 90.

4. I am indebted to Gillian Beer, who discusses the metaphors of knight-errantry and the sea in her chapter on *Beauchamp's Career* (*A Change of Masks*, 103 ff.).

5. See Donald Fanger, "Joyce and Meredith: A Question of Influence and Tradition," *Modern Fiction Studies,* 6 (1960):125–30.

6. Published in *Athenaeum* 2714 (1 November 1879), cited in Williams, ed., *Critical Heritage,* 207.

7. Stevenson's comments on Meredith are collected in Williams, ed., *Critical Heritage,* 520–22; for Henry James, see *Letters,* ed. Lubbock, particularly 2:258–66; for Thomas Hardy, "G.M.: A Reminiscence," in *Thomas Hardy's Personal Writings,* ed. Harold Orel (Lawrence: University of Kansas Press, 1966), 151–55; for Oscar Wilde, "The Decay of Lying," in *Intentions, Works* (New York: Lamb Publishing Co., 1909), 10:21–22, and "The Soul of Man under Socialism," in *Works,* 8:169.

8. Henry James, *Letters,* ed. Lubbock, 2:266.

9. Percy Lubbock, "A Final Appreciation," *Quarterly Review* 212 (April 1910); cited in Williams, ed., *Critical Heritage,* 517.

Selected Bibliography

PRIMARY SOURCES

1. Novels
   The entry cites the first book publication, with serialization data in parentheses. For later editions, see Michael Collie, *George Meredith: A Bibliography* (Toronto: University of Toronto Press, 1974). Particularly useful editions now in print are cited following the first editions.

The Adventures of Harry Richmond. London: Smith, Elder, 1871 (*Cornhill Magazine,* September 1870–November 1871).
   • Edited by L. T. Hergenhan. Lincoln: University of Nebraska Press, 1970.
The Amazing Marriage. London: A. Constable, 1895 (*Scribner's Magazine,* January–December 1895).
Beauchamp's Career. London: Chapman & Hall, 1876 (*Fortnightly Review,* August 1874–December 1875).
Celt and Saxon. London: Constable, 1910 (*Fortnightly Review,* January–August 1910).
Diana of the Crossways. London: Chapman & Hall, 1885 (*Fortnightly Review,* June–December 1884).
The Egoist. London: Kegan Paul, 1879 (*Glasgow Weekly Herald,* June 1879–January 1880).
   • Edited by R. M. Adams. Norton Critical Edition. New York: Norton, 1979.
   • Edited by George Woodstock. Harmondsworth, England: Penguin, 1979.
Emilia in England. London: Chapman & Hall, 1864 (*Revue des deux mondes,* November–December 1864). Second edition as *Sandra Belloni.* London: Chapman & Hall, 1886.
Evan Harrington. New York: Harper & Bros., 1860 (*Once a Week,* February–October 1860).
   • Edited by Barbara Hardy. Chicago: Academy Chicago, 1983.
Lord Ormont and His Aminta. London: Chapman & Hall, 1894 (*Pall Mall Magazine,* December 1893–July 1894).
One of Our Conquerors. London: Chapman & Hall, 1891 (*Fortnightly Review,* October 1890–May 1891).
   • Edited by Margaret Harris. St. Lucia: University of Queensland Press, 1975.

The Ordeal of Richard Feverel. London: Chapman & Hall, 1859 (*Revue des deux mondes,* April–May 1865).
  * Edited by John Halperin. World's Classics. Oxford: Oxford University Press, 1984.
Rhoda Fleming. London: Tinsley Brothers, 1865.
The Tragic Comedians. London: Chapman & Hall, 1880 (*Fortnightly Review,* October 1880–February 1881).
Vittoria. London: Chapman & Hall, 1866 (*Fortnightly Review,* January–December 1866).

2. Shorter Prose Fiction
The Shaving of Shagpat: An Arabian Entertainment. London: Chapman & Hall, 1856.
The Case of General Ople and Lady Camper. New York: John W. Lovell, 1890 (*New Quarterly Magazine,* July 1877).
Farina: A Legend of Cologne. London: Smith, Elder, 1857.
The House on the Beach. New York: Harper & Bros., 1877 (*New Quarterly Magazine,* January 1877).
The Tale of Chloe. New York: John W. Lovell, 1890 (*New Quarterly Magazine,* July 1879).

3. Poetry
Ballads and Poems of Tragic Life. London: Macmillan, 1887.
Jump-to-Glory Jane. London: Macmillan, 1889.
Last Poems. London: Constable, 1909.
Modern Love, and Poems of the English Roadside, with Poems and Ballads. London: Chapman & Hall, 1862.
Odes in Contribution to the Song of French History. London: Constable, 1898.
Poems. London: J. W. Parker, 1851.
Poems and Lyrics of the Joy of Earth. London: Macmillan, 1883.
Poems: The Empty Purse, with Odes to the Comic Spirit, to Youth in Memory, and Verses. London: Macmillan, 1892.
A Reading of Earth. London: Macmillan, 1888.
A Reading of Life. London: Constable, 1901.
The Poems of George Meredith. Edited by Phyllis B. Bartlett. New Haven: Yale University Press, 1978. A complete critical edition.

4. Essays and Miscellaneous Prose
An Essay on Comedy and the Uses of the Comic Spirit. London: Constable, 1897 (*New Quarterly Magazine,* April 1877).
Essays: On the Idea of Comedy; Homer's Iliad: A Review; St. Paul: A Review. London: Constable, 1898. Volume 32 of Constable's De Luxe Edition.
Miscellaneous Prose. London: Constable, 1910. Volume 23 of Constable's Memorial Edition.

The Notebooks of George Meredith. Edited by Gillian Beer and Margaret Harris. Salzburg and Atlantic Highlands: Humanities Press, 1984.

5. Collected Editions
Collected Works. 12 vols. London: Chapman & Hall, 1885–95. First collected edition of the novels.
De Luxe Edition. 39 vols. London: Constable, 1896–98; 1910–12. First collected edition of prose and poetry.
Memorial Edition. 27 vols. London: Constable; New York: Scribner's, 1909–11. Standard edition.

6. Correspondence
Cline, C. L., ed. *The Letters of George Meredith.* Oxford: Clarendon Press, 1970.

SECONDARY SOURCES

1. Bibliographies
Beer, Gillian. "George Meredith." In *Victorian Fiction: A Second Guide to Research.* New York: Modern Language Association, 1978.
Cline, C. L. "George Meredith." In *Victorian Fiction: A Guide to Research.* Cambridge, Mass.: Harvard University Press, 1964.
Collie, Michael. *George Meredith: A Bibliography.* Toronto: Toronto University Press, 1974.
Forman, Maurice Buxton. *A Bibliography of the Writings in Prose and Verse of George Meredith.* Edinburgh: Dunedin Press, 1922.
————. *Meredithiana.* Edinburgh: Dunedin Press, 1924.
Olmstedt, John Charles. *George Meredith: An Annotated Bibliography of Criticism 1925–1975.* New York: Garland Press, 1978.

2. Books and Parts of Books
Beer, Gillian. *A Change of Masks: A Study of the Novels.* London: Athlone Press, 1970. An outstanding discussion of Meredith's technique, stressing his artistic experiments and making use of unpublished material in the Altschul Collection of Yale University.
Bernstein, Carol. *Precarious Enchantment: A Reading of Meredith's Poetry.* Washington, D.C.: Catholic University of America Press, 1979. A subtle study disclosing a complexity in Meredith's verse overlooked or denied by earlier critics.
Buckley, Jerome. "George Meredith: Histories of Father and Son." In *Season of Youth: The Bildungsroman from Dickens to Golding.* Cambridge, Mass.: Harvard University Press, 1974. Focuses on the autobiographical

elements in *Richard Feverel* and *Harry Richmond* and indicates Meredith's indebtedness to earlier models of the bildungsroman.

Fletcher, Ian, ed. *Meredith Now: Some Critical Essays.* New York: Barnes & Noble, 1971. A collection of important recent essays. See Kettle, Lucas, Mitchell, and Tompkins entries under "3. Articles" below.

Halperin, John. "George Meredith." In *Egoism and Self-Discovery in the Victorian Novel: Studies in the Ordeal of Knowledge in the Nineteenth Century,* 195–214. New York: Burt Franklin, 1974. Examines Meredith's psychological insights in connection with his evolutionary worldview.

Henkle, Roger B. "Meredith and Butler: Comedy as Lyric, High Culture, and the Bourgeois Trap." In *Comedy and Culture: England 1820–1900,* 238–95. Princeton: Princeton University Press, 1980. Discusses *Richard Feverel* and *The Egoist* as sophisticated "amoral" elitist comedy.

Kelvin, Norman. *A Troubled Eden: Nature and Society in the Works of George Meredith.* Stanford: Stanford University Press, 1961. A detailed study of Meredith's ideas and his intellectual milieu; less satisfactory as criticism of the novels.

Knoepflmacher, Ulrich. "The Intrusion of Tragedy: *The Ordeal of Richard Feverel* and *The Mill on the Floss.*" In *Laughter and Despair: Readings in Ten Novels of the Victorian Era,* 109–35. Berkeley: University of California Press, 1971. Sees *Richard Feverel* as a unified tragedy, free of Eliot's sentimentalism.

Lindsay, Jack. *George Meredith: His Life and Work.* London: Bodley Head, 1956. Emphasizes Meredith's political ideas from a doctrinaire Marxist position.

Moses, Joseph. *The Novelist as Comedian: George Meredith and the Ironic Sensibility.* New York: Schocken, 1983. Sees Meredith as an "opposing self," a precursor of the modern novelist.

Priestley, J. B. *George Meredith.* New York: Macmillan, 1926. An early, but stimulating and seminal study linking the novels to the author's fundamental anxieties and self-mistrust.

Pritchett, V. S. *George Meredith and English Comedy.* New York: Random House, 1969. A vigorous, sometimes overstated assessment of Meredith's temperament and art, seeing him as a perplexing mixture of showman, romantic, and intellectual.

Stevenson, Lionel. *The Ordeal of George Meredith: A Biography.* New York: Scribner's, 1953. *The* biography of Meredith, combining a wealth of information with a judicious analysis of his character and work.

Stone, Donald D. *Novelists in a Changing World: Meredith, James, and the Transformation of English Fiction in the 1880s.* Cambridge, Mass.: Harvard University Press, 1972. Makes a good case for Meredith's essentially Victorian sensibility, set against James's "modern" aestheticism.

―――. *The Romantic Impulse in Victorian Fiction.* Cambridge, Mass.: Harvard

University Press, 1980. Sees Meredith as a "Romantic in spite of himself."

Swanson, Donald R. *Three Conquerors: Character and Method in the Mature Works of George Meredith.* The Hague: Mouton, 1969. Focuses on *General Ople, The Egoist,* and *One of Our Conquerors* for a very detailed analysis of Meredith's technique.

van Ghent, Dorothy. "On *The Egoist.*" In *The English Novel: Form and Function,* 183–94. New York: Harper, 1953. Finds a lack of societal and spiritual context for the figure of Willoughby.

Williams, Ioan, ed. *Meredith: The Critical Heritage.* New York: Barnes & Noble, 1971. An excellent collection of reviews by Meredith's contemporaries, with a very useful introduction.

Wilt, Judith. *The Readable People of George Meredith.* Princeton: Princeton University Press, 1975. Stimulating, highly original analysis of the novels, tracing a subversive subplot between the author and the fictional reader.

Woolf, Virginia. "The Novels of George Meredith." In *The Second Common Reader.* 1932. Reprint. New York: Harcourt, Brace, 1960. A balanced assessment of Meredith's importance for the development of the novel, registering Woolf's respect for his "packed and muscular mind" but placing him with the "great eccentrics."

Wright, Walter F. *Art and Substance in George Meredith: A Study in Narrative.* Lincoln: University of Nebraska Press, 1953. A thematic introduction to the novels, limited in approach but very good at placing minor as well as major characters in Meredith's system of comedy.

3. Articles

Baker, Robert S. "Faun and Satyr: Meredith's Theory of Comedy and *The Egoist.*" *Mosaic* 9, no. 4 (1976):173–93. This and the following two articles emphasize Meredith's pre-Freudian insight into repression and sublimation, as illustrated by a dense network of suggestive metaphors.

———. "Sanctuary and Dungeon: The Imagery of Sentimentalism in Meredith's *Diana of the Crossways.*" *Texas Studies in Language and Literature* 18 (1976):63–81.

———. "Victorian Conventions and Imagery in George Meredith's *One of Our Conquerors.*" *Criticism* 18 (1976):317–33.

Bartlett, Phyllis. "The Novels of George Meredith." *Review of English Literature* 3 (January 1962):31–46. A judicious defense of Meredith's intrusions, philosophy, and wit.

Buchen, Irving H. "The Egoists in *The Egoist:* The Sensualists and the Ascetics." *Nineteenth-Century Fiction* 19 (December 1964):255–69. Analyzes the egoism in all major figures in *The Egoist.*

Friedman, Norman. "The Jangled Harp: Symbolic Structure in *Modern Love.*" *Modern Language Quarterly* 18 (March 1957):9–26. Seminal study of the complex image patterns in the poem, anticipating more recent critical approaches.

Harris, Margaret. " 'The Fraternity of Old Lamps': Some Observations on George Meredith's Prose Style." *Style* 7, no. 1 (1973):271–93. Illuminating study of Meredith's "hyperactive verbal awareness" contrasted with the styles of James and Woolf.

Harris, Wendell. "Sifting and Sorting Meredith's Poetry." In *The Victorian Experience: The Poets,* edited by Richard A. Levine, 115–37. Athens: Ohio University Press, 1982. A more generous evaluation of Meredith's poetry than Lucas's in *Meredith Now.*

Howard, David. "George Meredith: 'Delicate' and 'Epical' Fiction." In *Literature and Politics in the Nineteenth Century,* edited by John Lucas, 131–71. London: Methuen, 1971. A very valuable Marxist reevaluation of *Sandra Belloni, Vittoria,* and *Beauchamp's Career,* giving the last a high place in the Meredith canon.

Hudson, Richard B. "The Meaning of Egoism in George Meredith's *The Egoist.*" *Nineteenth-Century Fiction* 3 (1948):163–76. An early study of Meredith's psychological ideas linking the novel to his poetry and post-Darwinian view.

Kettle, Arnold. *"Beauchamp's Career."* In *Meredith Now,* pp. 188–204. Another stimulating Marxist view on this difficult novel; ascribes its flawed achievement to Meredith's social isolation.

Korg, Jacob. "Expressive Styles in *The Ordeal of Richard Feverel.*" *Nineteenth-Century Fiction* 27 (1972):253–67. Demonstrates Meredith's skill in handling many different voices to juxtapose a chaotic reality and "serenely ignorant theorists" and systematizers.

Lucas, John. "Meredith as Poet." In *Meredith Now,* pp. 14–33. A vigorous but excessively negative verdict on Meredith's verse, excluding only "Modern Love" and a few ballads from dismissal.

Mermin, Dorothy. "Poetry as Fiction: Meredith's *Modern Love.*" *ELH* 43 (1976):100–119. Shows how the poem makes use of fictional conventions and strategies, particularly the motif of the fallen woman.

Mitchell, Juliet. *"The Ordeal of Richard Feverel:* A Sentimental Education." In *Meredith Now,* pp. 69–94. Places the novel in the bildungsroman tradition and relates it to Rousseau and other educational theories.

Smirlock, Daniel. "The Models of *Richard Feverel.*" *Journal of Narrative Technique* 11, no. 2 (1981):91–109. Emphasizes the inadequacies of traditional genres as demonstrated in the novel, as well as the fallacies of system making in readers and protagonists.

———. "Rough Truth: Synecdoche and Interpretation in *The Egoist.*" *Nineteenth-Century Fiction* 31 (1976):313–28. Finds Meredith concerned with the tendency of language—and speakers—to simplify, immobilize, and distort truth.

Stevenson, Lionel. "Meredith and the Art of Implication." In *The Victorian*

Experience: The Novelists, edited by Richard Levine, 177–201. Athens: Ohio University Press, 1976. A graceful summation of Meredith's originality and artistic effectiveness by a prominent and devoted Meredithian.

Stevenson, Richard C. "Comedy, Tragedy, and the Spirit of Critical Intelligence in *Richard Feverel.*" In *The Worlds of Victorian Fiction,* edited by J. H. Buckley, 205–22. Cambridge, Mass.: Harvard University Press, 1975. Representative of a growing critical conviction that *Richard Feverel* is a unified and successful work, both comic and tragic.

Stewart, Maaga A. "The Country House Ideals in Meredith's *The Egoist.*" *Nineteenth-Century Fiction* 32 (1978):420–41. Focuses on the symbol of the country house for an incisive study of Willoughby's pastoral pretensions and sterile aestheticism.

Tompkins, J. M. S. "On Re-reading *Evan Harrington.*" In *Meredith Now,* pp. 114–29. Gracefully records the discoveries and aesthetic pleasures to be found in even a minor Meredith novel.

Index